STUDYING THE HUMAN CONDITION

Science, Human Science, History, Ethics, Arts, Religion

Russell Garofalo, Masahiko Iguchi,

Patrick Strefford, Noah McCormack

Table of Contents

Figures..5

Tables 5

Chapter 1 The nature of science..6

Part 1. Science and pseudo-science...6

The mysterious game of science   7

Scientific knowledge and the scientific method   8

The development of scientific knowledge: is the earth round?   10

Pseudo-science   12

The different sciences   13

Chapter 2 The Human Sciences 16

Part 1. Human observation...16

On being human   16

Observing human beings   17

Observation bias   18

Answer bias   20

Loaded questions   22

Predictions, expectations, and human action   23

Reactance   25

On irrational behaviour   26

Part 2. Measuring human thinking and action 27

Universal measurements   30

Measuring life using money   31

Non-monetary values   32

Part 3. Experimentation in the human sciences 33

The Milgram experiments   33

The Stanford Prison Experiment   35

Part 4. Certainty in the human sciences 36

Constant change as a law of human science?   37

Probabilistic human science   38

Sample size and probability   38

Large numbers at work in the insurance industry   39

Trends and laws   41

Part 5. Explaining human behaviour...44

Reductionism and holism   44

Understanding in the human sciences   46

Unintended consequences   47

The limits of economic rationality   48

The human sciences in review   50

Chapter 3 Determinism and freedom 52

Part 1. Determinism in the human sciences 52

The effects of genes, and of society and family   52

Two kinds of free will   54

Free will and responsibility   55

Chapter 4 The Historical Sciences 62

Part 1. Individual and social pasts......................................62

What is History?...63

Significance   63

Evidence   64

The functions of history   65

History and group identity   66

History and power   67

Overcoming national history   70

History and human nature   72

Explaining the present   72

Part 2. Methodology: How to study the past 74

Primary Sources   75

Primary source problems: Individual filters   75

Social Bias   76

Secondary Sources   79

Hindsight   79

Part 3 Bias and history 83

Topic choice bias   83

Confirmation Bias   84

National Bias   84

Overcoming bias with multi-factor histories   85

Part 4 Theories of History 87

Geographical determinism   87

Cyclical Theories   87

Linear Theories   88

Great Person Theories   88

Economic Determinism   89

Conclusion   90

Appendix to Chapter 4: Doing history: the end of Japan's Pacific War.................91

Chapter 5 Ethics and morality 96

Part 1. What is ethics?..96

Academic studies of ethics   97

Part 2. Moral reasoning 99

Coherence, consistency, and truth   100

Part 3. Moral relativism 104
  Relativism and human diversity   105
  Lack of foundations for universal morality?   106
  Against moral relativism   107
  Relativism and globalization   108
  Selfish human nature as a problem for universal morality   108
Part 4. Ethical frameworks 110
  Kantian ethics   112
  Utilitarianism   116
  Rule utilitarianism   120
  Conclusion   121

Chapter 6 The Arts 123
Part 1. Ubiquitous art 123
  Definition of fine art   125
  Criteria to be Art   126
  Revised Criteria to be Art   128
  Ready-made art   129
  Subjective Aspects of Art   131
  Objective Aspects of Art   132
Part 2. The functions of art..135
  Art and Self-development   135
  Art and Politics   135
  Art as a human universal   137
  Conclusion   140

Chapter 7 Faith and religion 142
Part 1. The meaning of faith..142
  Faith as part of human nature   144
  Faith and Religion: what's different?   145
  Religion and the Right to Religious Privacy   146
  Defining God   147
  Types of religious beliefs   148
  Religion and daily life   149
  Religion and Science   150
Part 2. The functions of religion 152
  The benefit of believing in something   152
  Religion and Ethics   153
  Religion and Politics   154
  The social functions of religion: community, understanding, meaning   155
  Modernity and religion   157
  Conclusion: Religious tolerance and understanding   158
Artwork credits 162

Figures

FIGURE 1 THE MILGRAM EXPERIMENT   33
FIGURE 2 THE LIBET EXPERIMENT.   57
FIGURE 3 MANIPULATED PHOTO OF STALIN.   68
FIGURE 4 1898 FRENCH CARTOON.   77
FIGURE 5 SURRENDER OF CHINESE FORCES AFTER THE BATTLE OF WEIHAIWEI   78
FIGURE 6 TECHNOLOGICAL CHANGE AND SOCIAL CHANGE   89
FIGURE 7 THE TROLLEY PROBLEM   118
FIGURE 8 FOUNTAIN   129
FIGURE 9 MARILYN MONROE BY ANDY WARHOL.   130
FIGURE 10 PAINTINGS REFLECTING MELAMID AND KOMAR'S SURVEY RESULTS   139

Tables

TABLE 1 SAME CONCEPT, DIFFERENT MEANINGS   14
TABLE 2 ANSWER VARIABILITY ACCORDING TO QUESTION TYPE   21
TABLE 3 OLYMPIC SUCCESS BY GOLD MEDALS   28
TABLE 4 OLYMPIC SUCCESS BY MEDAL COUNT   28
TABLE 5 OLYMPIC SUCCESS BY MEDALS PER CAPITA   28
TABLE 6 OLYMPIC SUCCESS BY WEIGHTED MEDALS / GDP   29
TABLE 7 OLYMPIC SUCCESS BY WEIGHTED MEDALS / TEAM SIZE   29
TABLE 8 VARIATIONS ON THE MILGRAM EXPERIMENT   34
TABLE 9 FAMOUS HISTORICAL FIGURES   72
TABLE 10 JAPANESE AND U.S. WARTIME POWER   80
TABLE 11 THE DECLINE IN VIOLENT DEATH THROUGH HISTORY   88
TABLE 12 BENTHAM'S CRITERIA FOR MEASURING PLEASURE AND PAIN   117
TABLE 13 SOCIAL CHANGE AND RELIGIOUS CHANGE   158

Chapter 1 The nature of science

Science does not give us the taste of the soup.
Einstein

Science is built with facts just as a house is
built with bricks, but a collection of facts
cannot be called a science any more than a pile
of bricks can be called a house.
Poincaré

Part 1. Science and pseudo-science

What makes something scientific? What is not scientific? What is a science, and how many different types of science exist? What are the major differences and similarities between them? Why is science important? Is science 100% true, and can we trust it completely?

In this chapter, we begin by looking at what it means for something to be "scientific". To do this, we compare the broad category of science with pseudo-science or "fake science", looking especially at the procedures that make knowledge "scientific". Then we sketch out the major categories of science, starting with the natural sciences. In particular, we consider the different categories of natural science, their inter-relationships, and the factors that make them "natural", rather than "human".

The mysterious game of science

Richard Feynman, a famous physicist, proposed a metaphor that we can use to show what it is like for us to understand something about the world scientifically. Imagine that you travel to a place and time that are unfamiliar to you—an alien world. The people there are playing a game that you don't know at all. You don't know the rules, and you can't communicate with the people, so they can't explain the game to you. All you can do is watch the game closely, as an observer. If you watch long enough, you are likely to start to get some ideas about how the game is played. You may start to feel confident that you understand what is going on, and that you can suggest some reasonable **hypotheses** about what the aims and rules are, and the different strategies that players use. By watching further, you may be able to work out that your first impressions were not quite right, and you may revise your hypotheses. Over time, your understanding is likely to deepen. All the same, you may not ever be able to obtain a complete understanding, perhaps because the game is too complicated. Alternatively, the human brain may be too limited to understand some things. Also, some aspects of the game may be impossible to directly observe, or even guess at from what can be observed.

Hypothesis

A proposed explanation of something, based on limited information, which is a starting point for further investigation.

Our relationship to nature or the physical universe is something like that of this person observing a game in an alien time and place. We have no ability to talk with trees and rocks and atoms. They are "playing a game" that we don't know. We are outside observers who must spend time paying attention or observing, in order to get some idea of what is going on. We have currently some idea about some of the rules. But we probably don't know all of the rules. More importantly, many situations are so complicated that we have no precise idea of what is happening, or what will happen in the future. Because we live in this uncertain world, science is what we do in order to find and clarify the unknown rules of the "game" of the physical universe.[1] Importantly, our attempts at systematic science are based on the assumption that the universe follows regular rules, rather than random processes!

---

[1] If you're interested, you can read *The Feynman lectures on Physics*, Volume 1, Chapter 2 at the California Institute of Technology homepage: http://www.feynmanlectures.caltech.edu).

Scientific knowledge and the scientific method

As Feynman says, science uses observation, to see what is going on. It also involves reasoning, to try and explain events. Further, in order to check if our reasoning is correct, it usually also involves experiments. These experiments will either confirm what we thought or show that what we thought was not correct. If our ideas were incorrect, then we must change them, and repeat the process of observation, hypothesis-making, and experimentation.

The scientific method

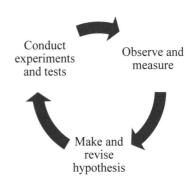

Conduct experiments and tests

Observe and measure

Make and revise hypothesis

At an individual level, you probably follow something like **the scientific method** every day. Consider, for example, that one morning, your smartphone doesn't power up. When you try to turn it on, nothing happens. This is an *observation*. Well, probably you think that this is a bit annoying. So, you ask yourself a *question*: "Why isn't my smartphone working?" This leads you to remember that you spent a lot of time watching videos before you fell asleep. So, you think, maybe the battery is flat. This is your *hypothesis*—a possible answer to your question—your phone is not working because it has no power. If that's the problem, then re-charging it, you think, should fix the problem. This *prediction* calls for you to do an *experiment*, to *test* your hypothesis. If your experiment leads to your smartphone powering up, then your hypothesis was probably correct: it is supported by the results of the experiment. If it doesn't, then maybe you'll need to do the same experiment again, but with a different power cable. And if that doesn't work, then you'll probably re-do the whole process from the beginning: think about what other problems may be affecting your non-working phone, come up with a new hypothesis, then make new predictions about

Experiment

A good experiment will focus on the possible effects of one factor at a time. E.g., to test the effects of a new anti-virus medicine on rats, you would need two groups of sick rats, which are identical and treated the same except that one group gets the medicine and the other doesn't. It will also measure relevant variables precisely, e.g., virus cell counts before, during, and after the treatment. Finally, other scientists must be able to repeat the results.

how you can test your hypothesis, then actually test it, and consider the feedback you get from testing. You may have to just take the smartphone back to the shop.

This is an everyday example of how the scientific process works. Of course, we wouldn't call this "science", but the procedure or process is "scientific". To be considered "science", in addition to the process, the topics and issues involved must be of wider interest. Also, they would need to be studied in experiments that can be repeated by other scientists, and that confirm the results. When the results are confirmed by other scientists, they will be recognized by communities of scientists. Over time, through repeated scientific observation, measurement, experimentation, hypothesis formation, and verification, the scientific community may develop a general agreement about what something is, and how it works. In such a case, that knowledge becomes *scientific* knowledge. Generally speaking, a piece of knowledge about one aspect of the world is a scientific *law*, while *scientific theories* are more general explanations of a phenomenon and may involve several laws.

Actually, within the scientific community, there is some debate about the exact conditions that must be met for something to be science. Some scientists, called *positivists*, say that unverifiable statements cannot be considered science. What is an unverifiable statement? Something like "God exists", or "Some stars in another universe are made of vanilla ice cream" might be examples of an unverifiable statement. Basically, we cannot show that they are true, or that they are untrue.

Another group of scientists prefer to follow the example of Karl Popper, who famously thought that verification was too difficult for many things, and that *falsifiability* was often enough. What Popper meant was that a scientific statement was one that could be disproved or *falsified*. For example, "No solids are liquids at the same time" could be disproved if we find a substance that shows two incompatible states at the same time. "Humans do not have extra sensory perception (ESP)", similarly, could be disproved by finding some people who have that ability. However, so long as we don't find exceptions to such scientific statements—so long as they are not falsified—we are justified in placing some trust in them, and we can call them "scientific".

Activity: The scientific process

- *Think of at least three well-established examples of scientific knowledge concerning the natural world (like gravity, for example). Choose one example and set out how the scientific process would work in that case (observation: hypothesis: test, etc.).*
- *Put the following parts of the scientific process in order:*
  a) Experiment   b) Hypothesize   c) Propose a law
  d) Measure   e) Observe   f) Re-experiment
  g) Make a theory
- *Explain how the following actions resemble scientific activity, as well as how they are different from scientific activity.*

A) Baking a cake using a recipe.
B) Collecting and organizing Pokémon cards.
C) Staying home because it looks cold and wet outside.
D) Investigating why a friend has stopped talking to you.
E) Studying your grandmother's face in order to draw a picture of her.
F) Baking a cake using your own imagination and feelings (no recipe!).

Unreliable science

Actually, not all science is "good science". In 2015, the academic journal *Nature* reported that when scholars tried repeating psychology experiments described in 100 scientific papers published in a range of academic journals, they were able to get the same results less than 40% of the time. Such low levels of replicability or repeatability are thought to affect chemistry, physics and engineering, medical science, and environmental science especially. One of the problems seems to be that as scientists try to achieve new and interesting results that will help them get better jobs and more research money, they tend to overlook data that looks uninteresting or which doesn't fit with their main hypothesis. Instead, they pay too much attention to data that looks interesting or which fits with their hypothesis. Another related problem is that academic journals also want to publish new and interesting papers, rather than papers that confirm what other experiments have shown. Bias obviously affects scientific study. This is why it is important that we try actively to challenge and even try to disprove the ideas that seem most attractive to us.

Today, the scientific field of replicability studies, which focuses on re-doing famous experiments to check if they can be trusted, is becoming more popular. Such studies will help to make science more scientific!

The development of scientific knowledge: is the earth round?

A well-known example of the development of scientific knowledge concerns the case of what people long ago thought about the shape of the earth. Early human beings on the earth were probably nomadic—they moved around in search of animals to hunt and plants to gather and eat. Those who lived on wide-open plains and grasslands, if they looked around or observed the earth as they roamed about, may have thought that the world was more or less flat. However, other people living near the sea may have made a rather different observation. They may have noticed that at sea, ships disappear into the horizon as they get further away. Not only that, but they disappear gradually, with the highest point remaining in view for the longest time. If the earth were flat, ships should just fade from view gradually because they become too distant to see. Thus, this observation may have led to the hypothesis that the earth is round. This hypothesis could be tested by experimenting with a boat. With the horizon being around 5 km for a small boat, people could measure when and how land disappeared from view, or the way in which other ships become visible at sea. The results of these experiments would support the idea that they earth is not flat, but round. Subsequently, modern technology has allowed us to verify this knowledge in various ways. For example, sailing around the world, or flying around the world, and taking pictures of the earth from space, are all ways in which the hypothesis of a round earth has been verified.

We have no basis for thinking that the earth is flat any more, and probably no one can seriously make this claim. However, it seems that the earth is not perfectly round either. The diameter of the earth across the equator (12,756km) is 42 km greater than the diameter of the earth between the poles (12,714km). This is known as equatorial bulge. The claim that the earth is round turned out to be closer to the truth than the claim that the earth is flat. But as further investigation is making clear, it is not true to say that the earth is perfectly round. Our understanding is deepening, but we have not, and may never, reach a complete understanding.

In this way, much scientific knowledge is based on induction. That is, we draw conclusions from observations that we have made. But we may notice new things, and discover that something we thought was true, is not. Then we would have to change what we think is true. Scientific truth is therefore something that is based on observation, reasoning, and experiment, and which has not been "proven wrong" through those processes. However, importantly, it has also not yet been "proven 100% right" either! The longer it stays unfalsified or not proven wrong, the more confident we may feel about its truth.

Activity: A limited truth

- *What are some generally accepted scientific truths? What are some exceptions to those truths? (For example, we tend to believe that it is true that water boils at 100 degrees centigrade. But actually, this is only true at sea level, for water with no impurities!) Is it likely that we know many truths that are always true for all times and places and conditions?*

Activity: Research and explanation

- *If the earth is moving around the sun at over 100,000 km an hour, how come it doesn't feel like we are moving?*
- *The earth spins faster than migrating birds fly. What happens when they fly west to east, in the same direction as the earth's rotation?*

Pseudo-science

A key difference between scientific and non-scientific knowledge is that scientific knowledge can be double-checked by doing experiments that could prove it correct or incorrect. In other words, any knowledge that cannot be checked is unscientific. Astrology, horoscopes, tarot card readings, graphology, Ouija board predictions and so forth are called pseudo-science because they pretend to be accurate, but do not follow the scientific method. For example, fortune-tellers may base their predictions on observations of the physical world. They might look at the position of the stars, for example, and relate them to a person's birthdate in making predictions about a person's life and fortunes. But for this to be accepted as "science", we would need to do some proper experiments. First, we'd need to investigate the fortune-teller's reasons for saying that there is a connection between stars and individual people. It is unlikely that the fortune-teller would be able to argue that there is a relationship based on verifiable or falsifiable claims. This would be established by other people in repeatable experiments.

Secondly, even assuming that the fortune-teller satisfactorily explains the relationship between stars and individual people's lives, and other scientists are able to verify this relationship, a second problem would probably occur. That is, most pseudo-science claims are "true" simply because they are so vague or so broad. For example, take a horoscope in a popular magazine that says "This will be a good week for Aries to find love." Given that there are hundreds of millions of Aries people on the earth, at least some of them may find love in that week and feel that the horoscope was true. Also, what does "find love" mean? Get married? Get a girlfriend/ boyfriend? Meet your best friend from high school? Meet your dog for the first time in a year? It could mean many different things to many different people. It is so vague that it has almost no meaning. But to be scientific, a claim must also be precise. A claim that is so imprecise that it must be true, again, is not scientific.

In conclusion, because they are not based on reliable evidence, because they are impossible to falsify and unrepeatable, and because they usually make claims that are so general that they are meaningless, astrology is pseudo-science. Of course, horoscopes and astrology are fun to read, and because most claims are so broad, they will be true for some people. But remember that they are far from being reliably true—they are just a kind of entertainment. We shouldn't use them as a reason for making decisions.

Activity: Evaluating claims

- *Which of these claims are "scientific"? Which are "pseudo-scientific"? Why? Refer to the possibility of falsifiability or testability, as well as the specificity of the claim.*
A) *People are selfish.*
B) *Some people are just born lucky.*
C) *Kit-Kats bring you good luck in exams.*
D) *Dogs can tell if you are sick by smelling you.*
E) *Impressionist art is much more beautiful than cubist art.*
F) *You can tell someone's personality from their blood type.*
G) *DNA tests can tell us something about a person's personality.*
H) *Aliens often come to earth, but the US, China and Russia have agreed to keep it a secret.*
I) *Smell is an important factor that affects whether you feel attracted to another person or not.*

The different sciences

It is possible to set out three types of science: natural, social, and human. They each focus on different primary concerns, or topics and questions.[2] Natural science, including physics, biology, and chemistry, examines, predicts, and explains natural phenomena. To do this, they use controlled experiments. They often use mathematical equations, as well as concepts whose meaning is not affected by historical, geographical, or socio-cultural contexts. Thus, chemical reactions and formulas such as $Na+Cl_2=NaCl$ or $E=mc^2$ and so on are everywhere the same.

Social science examines, predicts, and explains human behaviour and psychology, by looking at evidence such as actions and words, often gathered without full control over the situations in which they happen. Social sciences cannot do the same kind of controlled experiments that the natural sciences can. This is because the concepts and behaviours are considered to be affected by scientists studying them, as well as often being limited to particular times, places, and groups. For example, the study of religion involves observing what people do and say in real life with a focus on what is religious. But what is religious depends on where you are and how you understand religion. Is going to a shrine on the 1st of January religious? Is visiting a cathedral at Christmas time religious? The answer will vary for different people in different places. In this way, the meaning of religion can be very different for different people.

The broader category of human science focuses on how humans create *meaning* for their experiences. It looks at written texts and human actions over which

---

[2] Jerome Kagan, *The three cultures: natural sciences, social sciences, and the humanities in the 21st century*, Cambridge University Press, 2009.

scientists don't have much control, including novels, poetry, paintings, theatre, autobiography, and so on. In the case of fiction or autobiography, for example, writers tell us about people's inner feelings, beliefs, and emotions, which are inaccessible to the natural sciences, and hard to access via the social sciences. However, the concepts and behaviour considered in the human sciences are often limited to the contexts in which they take place, and it is often harder to generalize about the human sciences. This is a very important point about the human sciences. Of course, we can learn many things about what it means to be human, and how different humans may think, feel and act in different situations. But, it is very difficult to make general rules about humans using human science.

The different sciences use different types of evidence when making claims, and they have different amounts of control over gathering evidence. They also each have their own concepts which have meanings specific to them, even though vocabularies are sometimes shared. Let's look at the following example concerning the human emotion of fear.

Table 1 Same concept, different meanings

Science	Fear
Biology	Blood flows, electrical currents and chemical release in the brain and body, related to certain stimuli.
Social science	Terrorism or war are sources of collective worry or insecurity.
Human science	Poems, songs, novels, dance may express subjective feelings of fear.

Social and human sciences are affected by social conditions more than natural sciences are. Natural scientists prefer to focus on material or physical processes more than social, historical, and cultural factors. On the other hand, human and social scientists prefer not to give biology too much importance. Incidentally, in the medieval and early modern eras, the divisions between natural, human, and social science did not exist. Rather, all things were thought to be connected to each other, as indeed they are, and scholarship was more integrated. However, as human knowledge increased, the sciences became increasingly specialized and separate. For our purposes, in this text, we are classing the social and human sciences together, as a unified category.

Activity: What is a human being?

- *How might approaches from the different sciences try to respond to this question differently? A person is…*
    - *A) Chemistry:*
    - *B) Physics:*

C) *Biology:*
D) *Sociology:*
E) *Economics:*
F) *Anthropology:*

Activity: Is there a hierarchy of sciences?

- *Do you think people are more likely to be convinced about something—say, the nature of insanity—proven (they are told!) by a complex mathematical equation relating to genetic inheritance, or by something written by a poet or sung by a singer about the experience of being crazy, or by a social science study that considers how concepts of sanity and insanity are created by people in society?*
- *Would you be more likely to believe a neuro-science study, or a social science study?*

Chapter 2 The Human Sciences

Noah McCormack

This chapter clarifies what makes the human sciences "sciences" similar to the natural sciences, as well as what makes them "human" and different from the natural sciences.

Basically, the human sciences, which include economics, politics, sociology, history, anthropology, and so on, try to understand and explain human beings and the social, political, economic, and cultural environments that they exist in. To do this, they use a wide range of approaches, including surveys, statistical analyses, observation, experiments, and case studies. In this sense, they may sound similar to the natural sciences. However, what makes the human sciences very different to the natural sciences is that humans are the topic of investigation. As an object of study, humans are rather special.

Part 1. Human observation

Activity: Are humans special?

How are humans different from animals (plants), as well as from inanimate things (such as rocks, rivers, air)? How might those characteristics make scientific study focused on humans difficult? Come up with a few examples:

A)
B)
C)
D)
E)

On being human

You may think that humans are special because we have a sense of self, and that we are conscious, or aware of our own existence. Equally, you may point out that humans are able to imagine what other people are thinking. Empathy is the ability to understand the position of others, to understand the feelings of others. Consequently, we are aware that what we think and feel is not necessarily what others think and feel.

Obviously, these are not qualities of inanimate objects like rocks and atoms, or even of living things like trees and bacteria. At the same time, we should recognize that other animals may also have these abilities. It seems that at least some types of monkeys are able to recognize themselves in the mirror ("the mirror test") and so have a sense of self. Many pet owners believe that their dogs are able to sense what they are thinking. However, sense of self and empathy are likely much more highly developed in the case of humans. Let us take a few examples.

Say you have a dog at home, and today, it refuses to eat lunch. It hasn't been fed so it should be hungry. Why isn't it eating? The answer, surely, is that it is not feeling well. But take the same action in the case of a good friend at the university cafeteria at lunchtime. The answer to the question "Why not?" may be that she or he is not feeling well. But it could also be that they are trying to lose weight, or that they've decided not to eat in public, or that they don't like what is available, or that they woke up late and have just had breakfast, or that their religion has rules against eating during daylight hours, or that they have no money, or that they are planning to have a huge dinner at an all-you-can-eat restaurant, and so on. There are a huge number of possible reasons why someone does something, relating to their situation and how they understand it. In contrast, your dog's rejection of its lunch is unlikely to involve any complicated reasons.

Most of the non-human world follows **instinct**. But while some things in the human world are like that, many things are not. Our motives for action are much more complicated. What we do may be affected by economic motives or political ideologies, personal desires or social norms, ideas we encounter in media or our friends' opinions. Frequently, these things cannot easily be identified. Human observation is a very complex matter.

Instinct

Inborn and usually fixed patterns of behaviour in response to certain stimuli.

Observing human beings

Remember that scientific study involves observing and measuring a phenomenon. Based on observation and measurement, scientists develop hypotheses about what is happening and why. To test a hypothesis, they may do a number of experiments. Based on the results of the experiments, their hypothesis might be confirmed. If so, that knowledge will be considered more certain. Alternatively, the results may be inconclusive, meaning that the experiment didn't prove or disprove the hypothesis and more work will need to be done. Or, the results may contradict the hypothesis, suggesting that it was wrong. In this case, more observation, measurement, and further experiments will be necessary.

In human and social science, it is possible to observe people's actions and speech, but we cannot yet look inside people's minds to see what they are thinking. Of course, unlike in the natural sciences, we can ask questions of people, to try and find out. However, there are a few major problems with these procedures in the case of the human sciences. The first is that observation and measurement may affect what we are observing and measuring. A second is that people's answers to questions may be affected by bias and dishonesty.

Observation bias

In the case of physical objects, such as rocks or atomic particles, as well as many living things, what we observe is indifferent to us, meaning that it doesn't react or respond to us. Rocks, chemicals, and many living things don't notice or care about our observation. However, this is not the case for humans. When we observe others, we may change their behaviour, or we may not. It is very difficult to tell whether we have done so, just by observation!

This is called the "observer effect", and it happens because we are self-aware sociological animals. If we notice someone watching us, we try to put ourselves in their shoes. We try to imagine what they are thinking and respond appropriately. Imagine that you're chatting with friends at the back of a large classroom during a lecture. Suddenly, you notice the teacher looking right at you. What do you think and what do you do? Probably, you imagine that the teacher is looking at you and thinking that you are rude and disruptive. What would you do in such a case? That depends on how you feel, and what kind of person you are! If you want to show the teacher that you aren't a bad student, you may silently mouth "Sorry" to the teacher and become quiet. If you want to show your friends that you're not the type of person who thinks much of a teacher's opinion, then you may keep on chatting, or start sleeping.

The looking glass self

C.H. Cooley (*Human nature and the social order*, Scribner's, 1902) wrote about how we develop a sense of self by interacting with others and seeing ourselves through their eyes. Others are the mirror—the looking glass—through which we see ourselves.

The problem is that while observation may affect people's actions, it's hard to know (a) if it did, and (b) if it did, then in what way, and how much. Even if some students became quiet after noticing the teacher watching them talking during class, it is not certain that observation caused the students to become quiet. Even repeating the same observation of the same people in similar conditions may not give us an answer. Since people's behaviour is affected by their thoughts and feelings, and these vary constantly, a student who is chatty one day will not necessarily be chatty on another day, even in the same classroom with the same teacher and the same friends, and someone who is sensitive to being observed in one situation may not be so sensitive in another.

Activity: Being observed

● *Think of an experience when you suddenly noticed that someone was watching you. How did you react?*
● *Think of an experience when someone noticed that you were watching them. How did they react?*

Overcoming the observer effect

To overcome the problem of the observer effect, we could try to secretly observe people. This means that we could try to observe without the people becoming aware that they are being observed. This may be done by watching people from a distance as they interact in public spaces, for example. Another more recent approach is to collect big data from IT companies such as Facebook and Google, which provide data about people's search history and uploads. In these cases, people don't know that they are being observed (indirectly of course!), and so don't modify their behaviour.

It is also possible to make people used to being watched. Anthropologists who do fieldwork usually do it over a long period of time, so that the people they are studying get used to their presence, and "act naturally". Reality television shows may also overcome the observer effect by getting people used to being watched, although it seems more likely that the they are actually interested in *causing* the observer effect. Reality TV shows want the participants to change their behaviour and behave in strange and silly ways because they think will make for more entertaining television. Perhaps we should really call these TV shows, "unreality TV". None of these approaches is perfect, however.

Activity: Observation bias

A) *Is there a difference between singing in a one-person karaoke booth, and singing in a large karaoke room in front of lots of others?*
B) *If a teacher watched everything you wrote during a test, do you think that would affect your performance?*
C) *In some cities in the USA, police officers wear body cameras that record all of their interactions with members of the public. Make a hypothesis: What effect, if*

any, would you expect this to have on the police officers? How would you test your hypothesis?

Answer bias

The second problem concerns what happens when we ask people questions. In the human sciences and social sciences, we can ask people questions about what they do and why they do it, what they believe and why, and so on. However, there are several problems with this kind of method. Basically, people are unlikely to answer the simple truth. Rather, their answers are likely to vary according to the topic, the type of question, their feelings about the topic, what they think they should say, who the questioner is, and so on.

People may answer simple questions relatively truthfully. Questions about which toothpaste they use, or what car they drive may be easy for people to answer in a truthful way. But asking people questions about their use of drugs or how many people they have had sex with is more complicated. People may think that drugs are illegal, and so answer zero even if they have used them. Western studies indicate that between 30% and 70% of people who have used cocaine or opium-based drugs deny it when they are asked about it. On the other hand, people with no sexual experience may feel embarrassed to say that they have no sexual experience, and so they may answer, falsely, that they actually have had sex before. At the same time, people with lots of experience may feel embarrassed to say so, and answer, falsely, that they have less experience than they really do.

Above-average bias

A survey by the U.S. College Board of one million students in 1976-1977 found that 70% answered that their leadership skills were "above average", and only 2% below average. Would you expect Japanese college students to show similar results?

In these cases, the problem is that people's concern with how they look in the questioner's eyes, or how they look compared to what they think is "normal", makes them modify their answer. One survey of young men in the United States found that they said they preferred to date women who were physically attractive. But the women they actually dated did not match their reported preference. Living in a mass media society that is obsessed with beauty may have affected their answer, but it doesn't seem to affect their actions. What people say and what people do frequently does not match.

People's wish to be average is also another common factor that affects their answers. Most people are biased towards selecting a middle value rather than an extreme value when given a scale of choices between, for example, one and five. When a study asked people about their television viewing time per day, with two hours or more as the maximum value, only 16 percent chose it. But when two hours or more was the second of six choices, 37 percent of people chose it. Would the available options affect your answer choice?

Table 2 Answer variability according to question type

How much television do you watch each day?	None	<30 mins	30-60 mins	60-120 mins	>120 mins
How much television do you watch each day?	<120 mins	>120 mins	>180 mins	>240 mins	>300 mins

Another factor is that people who are being interviewed or surveyed may wish to please the questioner by telling them what they want to hear. Margaret Mead, a famous American anthropologist, was said to have been fooled by Samoan women who thought, because Mead seemed so interested in local sex practices, that it would be fun to pretend that they engaged in casual sex all the time, even though they didn't really do so.[3] The respective ages, genders, ethnicities, and personality matches of questioners in interviews are also factors likely to affect the answers that people give. Overall, these kinds of biases in the answers that people give to different types of questions mean that getting information from people directly is never a simple matter. People's answers may tell us more about the questions that were asked than about the people who answered the questions!

Activity: Answer bias

- *Write some questions that you think people are likely to answer truthfully. Write some more that you think people are likely to answer dishonestly. Mix them up, and get someone to answer them anonymously on moodle, with a note at the end about which questions were answered truthfully, and which were not. Were the responses as predicted?*

A)
B)
C)
D)

Activity: Self-evaluation and bias

A) *What are your strengths? What are your weaknesses? Compared to other students in the Faculty of International Relations, how would you position yourself? (1= higher, 2= average, 3= lower)*
B) *Make a chart showing where members of your group position themselves in terms of several strengths and weaknesses.*

---

[3] Derek Freeman, *Margaret Mead and the heretic: the making and unmaking of an anthropological myth*, Penguin, 1997.

C) *What can we conclude from viewing your group's chart about the manner in which people judge themselves?*

Loaded questions

A further point is that the people asking questions, as hinted at in the previous section, are also likely to have some biases. In fact, a value-neutral or non-biased approach to asking questions in the human sciences may be impossible. Consider the following example. In the 1990s, the Japanese Education Ministry directed that public schools in Japan should raise the *Hinomaru* flag and play the *Kimigayo* anthem on special occasions. However, because there was no law saying that these were the national flag and anthem, many people refused. In response, the government of the time passed a law making them officially the national flag and anthem and ordered schools to display the flag and play the anthem at graduation ceremonies and so on.

The type of question used to ask people their opinion about this series of events is likely to have a strong effect on their answer. If people are asked, "Do you think that the government should force children to become Japanese nationalists", the answer is surely more likely to be negative. If people are asked, "Do you think it is natural to teach children to respect their national flag and anthem?", then the answer is surely much more likely to be positive. Whether a totally neutral question is possible is unclear, but a more neutral question might ask something like the following. "Some people think (A) Children should be taught to respect their flag and anthem. Other people think (B) The government should not use its power to shape what children think about a particular flag and anthem. Which position, A or B, is closest to your position?

Activity: Question bias

● *Choose a controversial topic (euthanasia, Japan acquiring nuclear weapons, requiring children to be legally responsible for looking after their parents in their own age), and write three questions all asking the same thing, but in different ways so that one is more likely to lead to a positive answer, one to a negative answer, and one is relatively neutral.*

Abortion example

A) *Should unborn children have a right to life?*
B) *Should women have sovereignty over their own bodies?*
C) *What is your opinion on abortion? Is it permissible: (A) Always (B) Sometimes, (C) Never?*

A final consideration concerning observation and direct questioning is the fact that people do not always do what they say they will. At the same time, people often also do what they say they will not. Thus, there is likely to be always a considerable gap between what we can confirm by observation, and the explanations we can get by direct questioning!

Predictions, expectations, and human action

Another significant issue in the study of human beings is that when observing and interacting with people, we tend not to have a completely open mind. Rather, we tend to have certain expectations about what we are likely to observe, or what others are likely to do or say. Such expectations appear to have an effect on what other people do.

In terms of gender, for example, many parents' have prejudiced expectations of their children. They expect boys to do better at sports and girls to do better at tasks requiring careful neat work. Teachers are the same. Many teachers expect male students to be better at mathematics, and female students to be better at language-related tasks. Studies indicate that such everyday expectations lead to the formation of "self-fulfilling prophecies", in which expectations about what will happen, actually make those expectations come true. Using the previous example, boys may spend more time in sports and mathematics and take less care to be neat, because this is what is expected of them. Likewise, girls may be more careful to be neat and interested in literature but spend less time and effort on sports and mathematics, because this is what is expected of them. We could say that the expectations are making the paths, and the boys and girls are just following the paths that are made available to them.

In societies such as Finland and Sweden, these gendered expectations are relatively weaker, while they are relatively stronger in Japan or the U.S. Thus, they can have different results in different places. For example, one experiment required some American and Swedish women to read a short essay which said that women were not as good at mathematics as males, and others to read a neutral essay. After that, both groups did a mathematics test. American and Swedish women who read the negative essay both did worse than the group who read the neutral essay. This shows the power of expectations, and how self-fulfilling prophecies can work. But American women did much worse than Swedish women, probably because in Sweden, people are less inclined to believe that there are inherent or inborn differences of ability between men and women.[4]

---

[4] See, for example, Lee Jussin, *Social perception and social reality—why accuracy dominates bias and self-fulfilling prophecy*, Oxford University Press, 2012.

Another example comes from what is known as labelling theory, in the sociology of **deviance**. Deviance is acting in a way that is not considered normal, for example, having pink hair in a Japanese private junior high school, or breaking the law. However, people breaking the law is actually quite common. We all ride bicycles through stop signs, and drive cars faster than the speed limit, and look at mobile phones as we drive or cycle. Some of us drink and smoke when we are underage. Probably most of us fantasize about doing something illegal at one time or another. But despite all this, only a very few of us get labelled "deviant". Studies indicate that law-breaking members of poorer minority groups are more likely to be labelled negatively as deviants, while law-breaking members of the majority, and especially upper class wealthy people, are much less likely to be labelled deviants. This is partly the result of common *stereotypes* about criminals. We imagine criminality is more common in disadvantaged groups than in privileged groups. But treating some people as "deviant" and "criminally inclined" has the effect of raising their chances of engaging in more serious crime in the future. This is because it encourages other people to see them as a potential problem, and it encourages them to develop a self-image of themselves as a potential problem. These factors help to create a self-fulfilling prophecy.[5]

Deviance

Engaging in behaviour that goes against usually accepted standards, especially in social or sexual matters.

Stereotype

Commonly-held generalizations, often negative, about the members of a particular group. E.g., Americans are pushy and loud, Japanese are modest and polite, etc.

On a larger scale, we may consider the thesis outlined by Joseba Zulaika.[6] He points out that the US government's statement that al Qaeda was in Iraq before March 2003 was false—but once the US attacked Iraq based on this false logic and killed many thousands of innocent civilians and disrupted everyday life for an entire country—this statement became true. In this example of both a self-fulfilling prophecy and

Irony

A situation which is the opposite of what was intended or desired, and which therefore appears somewhat amusing or "interesting".

---

[5] Edwin Lemert, *Crime and deviance*, Rowman and Littlefeld, 2000.
[6] Joseba Zulaika, *Terrorism*, University of Chicago Press, 2009.

also *irony*, what the U.S. government said and did *produced* the reality of supporters of al Qaeda in Iraq.

Expectations and self-fulfilling prophecies are a concern for the human sciences on both macro- and micro- levels. We have a major effect on what others do. Indeed, what others do may be caused by us. Others may not have acted the way they did if we had held different expectations of them. To put it another way, it seems quite possible that the subjects of human science might behave differently with different researchers, because subjects react to the expectations and predictions of the researchers, who are all individually different.

Activity: Self-fulfilling prophecies and prediction bias

- *Are you one person when you are with some friends, and another person when you are with other friends? If so, do you think this has something to do with their expectations of you? Is there some kind of self-fulfilling prophecy at work?*
- *Is it good to have classes at university in which students are put into groups according to their English scores? What benefits does such a system offer? What kinds of problems might it give rise to? Which are more important, the pros or the cons?*

People's expectations affect what happens to stock market prices and real estate prices and financial markets, and so forth. If people believe bitcoin values will keep rising, they buy some. If enough people buy, then bitcoin values will actually rise. The opposite is also true. If people expect bitcoin values to drop, then they will tend to sell what they have, and if enough people do this, it will lead to a fall in bitcoin prices. This is why confidence is so important for financial markets. Expectations even affect people's responses to medical situations. People who are told that they are taking an effective medicine may get better, even though in reality they have been given a placebo or a dummy medicine that is not supposed to have any medical significance. It seems that positive people are more able to recover from illnesses than negative people. They have confidence, they expect they can, so they more often do.

Reactance

Of course, people do not necessarily try and meet all expectations and predictions. Being expected to do badly can push some students to do great things, because they want to prove to the person who didn't expect much of them that they were wrong. Being expected to be a model student because of teachers' past experience with older brothers and sisters can push students to react against that and be "bad students". If people feel that others are forcing them to take a certain position, then it seems that they sometimes react in a way that is the opposite of what is desired or expected. This is known as **reactance**.

One famous story is that when the US president changed from Kennedy to Johnson, the press predicted that he would get rid of all the people working in the White House who had been hired by the Kennedy government. Johnson famously reacted by inviting them all to stay. Another more widespread example is that people attracted to someone may find that their level of attraction rises if the target of their affection is cold and distant.[7] Some other everyday examples include the tendency for children to eat more vegetables if their parents forbid them to eat them. The ban limits their possible choices. Feeling this limitation as a decrease in their freedom of choice, they begin to want to eat the vegetables, even though they didn't want to eat them when they were asked to! Another is that if adults tell a young person who is inclined to smoke that they **must** smoke, that person becomes less inclined to smoke…

Activity: Reactance

- *Imagine that (a) your teacher tells you that you must do homework. What factors might encourage you to show reactance, or refuse to do it? Imagine that (b) your teacher says that they won't accept any homework from you ever again. Might this be more likely to make you show reactance?*
- *What is the significance of the psychological phenomenon of reactance for the human sciences in general? Consider, for example, the case of stereotypes about groups such as women / men, or national / ethnic / religious groups: When might they lead to reactance?*

On irrational behaviour

Some political and economic scientists assume that people know what they want and make rational decisions to achieve their desires. By assuming this, it becomes easier to make predictions about what they will do. However, it seems that people are often *irrational* actors. In addition to the issues outlined above, Daniel Kahneman has conducted a range of studies that show people are frequently irrational.[8] **Loss aversion** is when people think an object is more valuable when they have to give it up than when they get it. People often generalize from insufficient information, thus showing a tendency to be **overconfident**. People ignore evidence that doesn't fit with their beliefs—this is known as **confirmation bias**. People have **weak self-control**, and often give in to short-term pleasures that they know are bad

---

[7] Sharon and Jack Brehm wrote about this phenomenon of people resisting what they are expected to do in more detail in their book *Psychological reactance: a theory of freedom and control*, Academic Press, 1981.
[8] Daniel Kahneman, *Thinking, fast and slow*, Farrar, Straus and Giroux, 2011.

for them. Given these points, the rational actor model seems to be a fiction. It is not a good way to understand people. And if people are sometimes but not always rational, then logically, it will not be possible to predict their behaviour in precise ways. How do we know when they are rational and when they are not?

Part 2. Measuring human thinking and action

So far, we have outlined some of the difficulties of the human sciences. Humans are self-conscious and able to take the position of others, so that when they know they are being observed, they may change their behaviour. It is possible to ask people questions, but you cannot always trust people's answers, and in fact questions too, are likely to contain some form of bias. Not only that, but any study of humans that involves interaction with researchers will affect the way that people behave. This is because researchers have expectations and stereotypes about the people they are studying. Exactly what the effect may be is hard to say, however, as people may try to meet researcher expectations in some cases and try to deny or reject researcher expectations in other cases.

These issues do not make the study of humans impossible. They just make it rather complicated. Most studies try to simplify things by firstly focusing on what people do, rather than on what people think. This is because thoughts are hard to see, and it is even harder to isolate one thought from other thoughts and to quantify it. Of course, it is also true that what people do or say will not necessarily match what they are thinking, and human scientists will need to be careful when connecting what people do with interpretations of what people think.

Some human scientists may study what people do by observing them in the field to see how they spend their everyday lives, or by asking them questions about what they do, believe, trust, and so forth. Others like to use statistical data about consumer behaviour or voting patterns. In any case, though, one of the primary issues is how to measure what people are doing. With the metric scale, we can measure distance in mm, cm, m, km, and so on. It gives us a reliable standard measurement that we can use to compare and contrast the size of different things. But what should we use in the case of humans? Clearly, the answer depends on what we want to measure, and why we want to measure it. Data that involves mathematical or statistical figures may seem to be the most objective. But numbers are not everything.

One interesting example is the case of the Olympic Games. The mass media and many people in most countries become tremendously excited by performances *mainly by people of their own country* at the Olympics every four years. We can judge individual performances by comparing them to other competitors in the same event at the same games and in the past. But how to judge the results of a country overall is rather more complex. You may think that countries with the most medals, or countries with the most gold medals, are obviously the most successful. But there are other ways to think about this. You can find some interesting comparative data at the website here: http://www.medalspercapita.com.

In terms of overall medals and overall gold medals, the United States was clearly by far the most successful country at the 2016 Rio Olympics. However, the number of medals is not the whole story. After all, some countries have vast populations which are likely to provide more potential winners. Looked at in terms of medals per capita, the most successful countries start to look quite different.

Table 4 Olympic success by medal count

	Country	Medals
1	United States	121
2	China	70
3	Great Britain	67
4	Russia	56
5	France	42
6	Germany	42
7	Japan	41
8	Australia	29
9	Italy	28
10	Canada	22

Table 3 Olympic success by gold medals

Rank	Country	Gold
1	United States	46
2	Great Britain	27
3	China	26
4	Russia	19
5	Germany	17
6	Japan	12
7	France	10
8	South Korea	9
9	Italy	8
10	Netherlands	8

Given the tiny populations of countries like Grenada and the Bahamas, it is clearly a major achievement for them to win a medal of any kind. Given their success, despite having scarce population resources, these countries could be said to be much more successful in producing Olympic stars than bigger countries with many more people.

Table 5 Olympic Success by Medals Per Capita

Rank	Country	Medals	Population	Population per Medal
1	Grenada	1	106,825	106,825
2	Bahamas	2	388,019	194,009
3	Jamaica	11	2,725,941	247,812
4	New Zealand	18	4,595,700	255,316
5	Denmark	15	5,676,002	378,400

6	Croatia	10	4,224,404	422,440
7	Slovenia	4	2,063,768	515,942
8	Georgia	7	3,679,000	525,571
9	Azerbaijan	18	9,651,349	536,186
10	Hungary	15	9,844,686	656,312
45	Japan	41	126,958,472	3,096,548

If we give each country a score for their number of each type of medal (4 for gold, 2 for silver, 1 for bronze) and calculate a total score for each country, and then divide each country's GDP (in billions of USD) by their medal score, we obtain a measure of medals per country per GDP, or in other words, a rough measure of how the economic wealth of each country correlates to the number of medals that it won. Grenada comes out on top again.

Table 6 Olympic Success by Weighted Medals / GDP

Rank	Country	Weighted Medals	Gold (4)	Silver (2)	bronze (1)	GDP (Billion US $)	GDP per Weighted Medal
1	Grenada	2	0	1	0	0.82	0.41
2	Jamaica	32	6	3	2	15.07	0.47
3	Kenya	37	6	6	1	33.62	0.91
4	Fiji	4	1	0	0	3.81	0.95
5	Armenia	10	1	3	0	10.25	1.02
6	Georgia	14	2	1	4	14.37	1.03
7	Burundi	2	0	1	0	2.33	1.16
8	North Korea	16	2	3	2	22	1.38
9	Bahamas	5	1	0	1	7.79	1.56
10	Tajikistan	4	1	0	0	6.52	1.63
70	Japan	85	12	8	21	5867.15	69.03

To talk about success at the Olympics, even if it is based on apparently objective criteria such as the number of medals, becomes a complex matter when we include these other factors.

Table 7 Olympic Success by Weighted Medals / Team Size

Rank	Country	Weighted Medals	Gold (4)	Silver (2)	Bronze (1)	Team Size	Weighted medals per 100 athletes.
1	Tajikistan	4	1	0	0	7	57
2	United States	296	46	37	38	554	53
3	Kosovo	4	1	0	0	8	50

4	Jordan	4	1	0	0	8	50
5	Azerbaijan	28	1	7	10	56	50
6	Russian Federation	131	19	18	19	265	49
7	Jamaica	32	6	3	2	68	47
8	Great Britain	171	27	23	17	366	46
9	North Korea	16	2	3	2	35	45
10	Cote d'Ivoire	5	1	0	1	12	41
27	Japan	85	12	8	21	338	25

We can talk about the most efficient teams as being Tajikistan and the US, since their athletes obtained medals at a rate of over 50 medals per 100 athletes, or more than double Japan's rate. The criteria chosen for examination and comparison, in other words, determine what the results will be.

What we choose to measure is a key factor, and this will tend to what we think is important. (A) What are we measuring? Economy? Efficiency? Overall successes? (B) What are we comparing? Similar things, or different things? It will be necessary to be precise about the first point, and to remember to keep in mind whether it is justifiable to do the second…

Activity: In-class mini-project

- *Suggest at least ten criteria that could be used for ranking universities. Consider different points of view: students, parents, teachers, researchers, administrative staff, education ministries, accountants, banks, local and city governments, companies, etc.*
- A) *Which criteria are the most important? Why? Are different criteria biased in different ways?*
- B) *Is it possible to say, objectively, that there is a single "top" university anywhere in the world?*

Universal measurements

Just as the metric scale is considered by some to be a universal way of measuring distance, some scholars, especially economists, think that money may be a universal way of measuring the things that humans value. If everything can be calculated to have a money value, then we can use money to compare the value that people give to different things. Of course, it needs to be possible to calculate the monetary value of all things. Some things are easier to calculate than others. Consider the following items.

Activity: Monetary valuations

- *How could you calculate the value of the following in terms of money? Give at least two methods for each item.*
- A) *A child*
- B) *A good friend*
- C) *Pet dogs and cats*
- D) *University education*
- E) *Living without the threat of nuclear catastrophe*
- F) *An environment free of dangerous levels of pollution*

Measuring life using money

Obviously, one problem with this kind of measure is that the same thing may have different value to different people. A single organization may give different value to something like a human life, depending on whose life is involved. Consider that in 1999, the United States Air Force bombed the Chinese Embassy in Belgrade. Whether this was a mistake or intentional is still debated. The attack killed three Chinese reporters and injured 27 other people. Each victim's family received around $150,000 in condolence payments. However, in the early 2000s when US forces killed civilians in Afghanistan, the condolence payments were limited to less than $2,500 or one-sixtieth of the amount paid in the case of the Chinese Embassy in Belgrade. Both of these estimations of the value of a human life were, however, dramatically low compared to the $1.8 million paid to each of the families of those killed in the 2001 World Trade Centre Bombings (the September 11 terrorist attacks).

Money may measure the value of some things, but in these cases, it seems to be telling us that what a life is worth is highly subjective. It varies according to the economic level of the country in which that life takes place (which is connected to people's ability to have life insurance, for example). It may also depend on the power relations of the countries involved, with powerful countries having more ability to get away with only giving low payments to others, and to obtain high payments from others.[9] At a more local level, the values of lives vary according to age, and whether the person has a paid job or not. It may also vary according to popularity or health.

Activity: The variable value of human life

- *Research insurance pay-outs for accidental deaths of young, medium, and old men and women in Japan. What do your results suggest about the value of human life (or, the different values of different human lives)?*

---

[9] See Marc W. Herold "The Matrix of Death: (Im)Precision of U.S Bombing and the (Under) Valuation of an Afghan Life" RAWA News, October 6, 2008.
http://www.rawa.org/temp/runews/2008/10/06/the-imprecision-ofus-bombing-and-the-under-valuation-of-an-afghan-life.phtml

Non-monetary values

At the state level, Jerome Kagan has calculated that the percentage of U.S. GDP spent on health increased 300% between 1958 to 2000 (from 5% to 15%). During this time, the average person's lifespan increased from 68 years to 77 years, a gain of 14%. In money terms, for the entire U.S. population, each year of life after 68 years of age cost some 100 billion dollars, he writes. Was this reasonable? It's impossible to say, Kagan says, because money spent and the psychological situation of having an extra year of life cannot be easily compared.[10]

We must say that some things cannot be measured in money, or even if they are, the meaning of that monetary value is limited. Let's take as an example the money it costs to raise a child from birth to adulthood. In Japan, Benesse suggests the average cost of raising a child until 22 years of age is 16 million yen, with another 10 million yen at least needed for school and university costs. But to many parents, this monetary consideration is not that important compared with the satisfaction of living with a child for several decades. It is simply not possible to compare having a child with having 26 million yen, because the two things are not comparable. Of course, this doesn't mean that money is not important at all, however. Many parents report wanting more children than they actually have. This suggests that money, as well as probably work obligations, does have some effect on the total number of children that parents have.

Money may seem to provide a measurement standard that is universal and objective, but like with Olympic medals, that objectivity seems to fade away on closer inspection. People's sense of what is valuable varies, and people's sense of how valuable things are also varies. Perhaps rather than trying to understand something using just one measure, it is better to try and understand using multiple different measures. This is because, after all, each thing tends to have multiple dimensions, and so one measure is insufficient.

Activity: Measuring social phenomena

● *Suggest several different ways to measure each of the following:*
A) Social class / level
B) Intelligence / stupidity
C) Happiness / sadness
D) Economic conditions
E) Political conditions
F) Madness / sanity

---

[10] Kagan, *op. cit.*

- *What do your measures suggest about the nature of these various factors and conditions that you are measuring?*

Part 3. Experimentation in the human sciences

In the natural sciences, experiments are a key part of the scientific method. This is also true in the human sciences, but experiments are more difficult and so less common in the human sciences. It is, after all, much easier to isolate atoms or chemicals or individual animals and experiment on them in controlled conditions than it is to isolate a human being and experiment on it in controlled conditions. In an experiment, the thing being studied is called the subject. Even if you can control what happens to the subject in a laboratory experiment, there is still the problem that every subject has an individual and unique background and personality. To fully control for all of those outside factors is virtually impossible. Not only that, putting people into a laboratory is itself making them do something in an artificial environment. This will change their behaviour, and so we cannot be sure that the way people behave in the laboratory experiment will be the same as how they will behave in the real world.

Activity: Research plan

- *How do you think you could investigate the relative influence on individual personality formation of (a) genetics / DNA and (b) the environment in which people grow up? Why would it be difficult to do such an experiment? Is it possible to investigate the interaction of genetics and environment?*

The Milgram experiments

In the 1960s, Stanley Milgram conducted some experiments at Yale University in the United States. One of the questions that he was interested in was why highly educated and civilized German bureaucrats had helped the Nazi regime to kill millions of people, including Jewish, non-heterosexual, Roma, and disabled people, during the 1940s. After the war, many people who had done these war crimes said they had simply "followed orders". Milgram wanted to investigate this. Could someone powerful order ordinary people to ignore their conscience and harm others? To research this

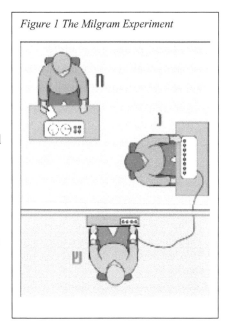

Figure 1 The Milgram Experiment

question, he set up an experiment (which no university would ever permit today on ethical grounds!) in which three people were involved. One was a real scientist, one was a "learner" (actually an actor), and another was a "teacher"—the subject of the experiment. The subjects were hired via newspaper advertisements and paid for their time.

The subjects were told that their role in the experiment was to help investigate the effects of punishment on learning. The subjects were to read out a list of words to a "learner" who was in a different room, and then ask the learner a question about the words. If the learner made an error, the teacher pressed a button to give them an electric shock. Additional errors led to stronger shocks, meaning that the more times the learner made a mistake, the stronger the electric shocks were. Although the teacher could not see the learner, they could hear the learner (an actor) make painful sounds as the shocks increased in strength. Of course, the learner did not really receive the electric shocks, they just pretended to. Although many teachers said that they would like to stop giving the shocks as they heard the "learner" make sounds of pain, all of them continued to 300 volts, and two-thirds went to the maximum 450 volts.

The role of the real scientist was to push the teacher to give shocks. The scientist, as the powerful authority figure, told the teachers that they were teachers, insisted that the experiment should come first, that no lasting harm would come to the learners, and ordered teachers to do their duty and keep on with the experiment.[11]

In the experiment, most teachers (636 participants in total) kept on giving the shocks right to the end. In this way, they did their duty, as teachers, as told to by the authority figure, the scientist. Milgram concluded that the German bureaucrats who participated in the mass killings by the Nazi regime were ordinary people, rather than evil individuals. He thought that the experiment showed almost anybody could be "forced" or "pressured" to do harm to others in the name of science. It showed that people would ignore their conscience and obey a legitimate authority who said that they would take responsibility for what happened. Needless to say, this was a shock for many people.

Table 8 Variations on the Milgram Experiment

Altered variables	Obedience level
Ordinary person instead of scientist	20%
Experiment site in rundown offices (not university)	47.5%
Two teachers, with the subject instructing another to give the shocks	92.5%

[11] You can watch a dramatized version of the experiment made by Milgram at the following link. https://www.youtube.com/watch?v=WXfgA-cvCWA.

Teacher has to press learners' hands on electric shock plate	30%
Other teachers refuse to give shocks	10%
Scientist communicates via telephone from another room	20.5%

Activity: Reviewing the Milgram experiments

- *Why was this experiment controversial? Was it a "good experiment"? Did it show what Milgram thought it showed? Is it reasonable to generalize from people in the experiment to people in general, and to Nazi death camp workers?*

The Stanford Prison Experiment

Another famous human science experiment is the so-called Stanford Prison Experiment, in which a mock-prison was established at Stanford University in California under psychologist Philip Zimbardo. It was run by student volunteers who received the equivalent of around $100 a day in today's money. Recruited via a newspaper ad that promised money for participation in a prison experiment, twelve students were selected at random to be guards, and another twelve to be prisoners. Zimbardo first gave the students psychological tests because he wanted to choose students who were as "normal" as possible.

In the orientation for the guards, Zimbardo told guards that they were allowed to use fear and boredom to control the prisoners, but not physical violence. Guards dressed and were equipped as guards, and were given dark sunglasses, while prisoners were dressed as prisoners, chained up, and called by numbers rather than names to depersonalize them.[12]

As the experiment went on, many of the guards abused their authority and became quite sadistic, meaning that they got pleasure from causing pain to the prisoners. The prisoners tended to become very negative and "giving up", accepting their position as inferior beings. Some were highly traumatized, and even seemed to "go crazy", in the words of Zimbardo. Zimbardo was a participant in the experiment as the supervisor of the prison, and also the designer of the experiment. Perhaps because of this, he ignored the trauma of the prisoners and continued the experiment for too long, according to critics. Conditions became so bad in the "prison" that the experiment was stopped earlier than planned.

Activity: Reviewing the Stanford Prison experiment

- *Can you see signs of experimenter expectations playing a role in this experiment?*

---

[12] This link has some footage: https://www.youtube.com/watch?v=RpDVFp3FM_4. The experiment was written about in detail in Philip Zimbardo, *The Lucifer effect—understanding how good people turn evil*, Random House, 2007.

- *Is it likely that certain types of personalities, and not others, will be attracted by an advertisement calling for participation in a prison experiment?*
- *Do you think it is possible to propose any laws about human nature from this experiment?*
- *The Nuremberg Code summarized below sets out ethics guidelines for experiments involving humans. Would these two experiments have been approved?*

Summary of the Nuremberg Code on experiments involving human subjects

- *Human subjects must be volunteers, well-informed, and understand the experiment.*
- *Subjects must not experience unnecessary physical and mental suffering and injuries.*
- *The human subjects must be free to immediately leave the experiment at any point when they feel physically or mentally unable to go on.*
- *Medical staff must stop the experiment at any point when they think that continuation would be dangerous.*

The Helsinki Declaration

(The **Helsinki Declaration** is a similar, more detailed code of ethics for experiments)

- *The wellbeing of subjects must come first.*

Part 4. Certainty in the human sciences

The ultimate aim of science is said to be to develop increasingly certain knowledge about the world. In the human sciences, this might mean, for instance, that we become able to make laws and theories about what people are like. This raises several questions. The first is, can we actually have certain knowledge about human behaviour? Do the Milgram or Stanford Prison experiments, for example, tell us about universal human behavioural rules and tendencies, or about what certain people in those conditions will do? Are these experiments repeatable? Are the experiment conditions sufficiently well-controlled? Do these experiments help us to make laws and theories about human beings?

Activity: Universal laws in the human sciences

- *Can you think of any laws about human behavior that apply for all people everywhere all of the time?*
- *If there are any such laws, what would those laws imply, in terms of human nature? Would they mean that we are not free?*

Constant change as a law of human science?

Marvin Minsky, a famous scientist who was a pioneer in the field of artificial intelligence, suggested that human psychology was different to physics. Mainly, it was much more difficult! His explanation was that physics was able to identify simple laws that were valid in all situations and times. By contrast, Minsky thought that this was not the case of human brains, which were constantly self-correcting and changing so that what was the case one day would not be the case another day.[13] It seems quite likely that our economies, societies, and political systems are pretty much the same: they are a complex set of self-adapting systems that are constantly in interaction with other systems. Because of this, no simple laws will ever hold true for humans.

In short, inanimate objects and most animals and plants are not self-aware, so they don't modify their behaviour according to what they know and what they think. But humans are self-aware, constantly learn new things, and we are not natural or innocent in our actions. That is, we can know what we do, and we can know why we do what we do. From that knowledge, we get the freedom to choose whether we keep on doing what we do. This is what Minsky means by the human brain being self-correcting and constantly changing. Seth Stephens-Davidowitz expands this idea to say that societies and politics and economies are also self-correcting and constantly changing.[14] Therefore, it is pretty difficult, if not virtually impossible, to set out laws that will be true for everyone all of the time. Human science laws and theories, therefore, tend to be a little different from natural science laws and theories.

Activity: Human science claims and natural science claims

A) *All human societies are hierarchical.*
B) *Hungry people are generally unhappy.*
C) *Usually, when a product's cost increases, fewer people will buy it.*
D) *First-born children tend to be more successful than later-born children.*
E) *Most boys feel an unconscious attraction to their mothers, and are jealous of their fathers, while most girls feel an unconscious attraction to their fathers and are jealous of their mothers.*
● *What are some famous natural science laws and theories? How are they different to the laws and theories outlined above?*

---

[13] Marvin Minsky, *The society of mind*, Simon and Schuster, 1988.
[14] Seth Stephens-Davidowitz, *Everybody lies: big data, new data, and what the internet can tell us about who we really are*, Bloomsbury Publishing, 2017.

Probabilistic human science

It should be clear to you that the laws above contain numerous qualifiers such as **tend to be**, **most**, **usually**, **generally**, and so forth. This is because it is almost impossible to make definite 100% true claims about all people. Human science laws are not definite for all people and all time. Rather, they are probabilistic in nature. This means that we talk of "most people", "a small percentage of people" and so forth in the human sciences. We can make predictions about people, but they will be probabilistic predictions, rather than definite predictions. This means that they will apply to many of the people in a group, but not all.

Activity: Probabilistic predictions

A) *In Japan, in late March of their fourth year of their studies, X% of students will graduate, and Y% of students will not graduate.*
B) *In Japan, in early April following graduation, A% of new graduates will begin work, and B% of new graduates will not.*
- *What other probabilistic predictions can you think of? What are they based on?*
- *If you toss a coin ten times, what does probability theory (mathematics) predict? If we do it in class and note the outcome (heads or tails), what kinds of results will we get? If we make predictions based on your outcomes, what may happen?*

Sample size and probability

If we look at individual coin toss results, they should be relatively varied. Some people (A) may have more heads, and other people (B) may have more tails, and a few people (C) may have an equal number of heads and tails. If we only had the data from people A or people B to make predictions with, it is likely that we would make some bad predictions. Of course, data from people C would make it possible for us to make mathematically justified predictions. But by putting everyone's results together, we should be able to get close to the mathematically predicted average of around 5 heads and 5 tails per 10 tosses. This is because the random variations—people who get more tails and people who get more heads—should cancel each other out and become unimportant.

The more results we have, the more the unusual results (more heads, more tails) should cancel each other out, with the overall average becoming closer to the "real probability." Obviously, with something simple like a coin toss, we can mathematically calculate the real probability. But with other things that are more complicated, we may need to actually measure what happens in society, in large enough numbers that we can be sure of obtaining a relatively reliable average score indicating how often something should happen. This principle, according to which random variations should cancel each other out given enough trials or samples, is known as **the law of large numbers**.

Activity: The Law of Large Numbers

● *Explain how and why the law of large numbers is important to the following:*
A) *Insurance companies (accident rates)*
B) *Airline ticketing offices (no-show rates)*
C) *Local governments and school boards (birth rates)*
D) *University entrance boards (student acceptance rates)*

Activity: Sibling numbers as a large numbers example

		Individual	*Group*	*Class*	*Year*
Household children by sex	*Female*				
	Male				

● *Calculate (a) the number of female and male children in the household that each student was raised in, (b) combine data for all students in small groups, (c) combine data for the entire class, (d) combine data for all classes. If we perform this operation, will the results tend to confirm the law of large numbers? Are there some biases that we should control for?[15]*

Large numbers at work in the insurance industry

Believing that the risk of a car crash occurring is 1% (1 crash per 100 drivers), an insurance company might sign up 100 people to cover that claim (one $10,000 car is 100 dollars $+\alpha$ per client). With such a small pool of clients (100), however, things could go very wrong—they could end up with an accident rate of 3% or even 10%, simply because of random variations in their small sample! Thus, that company might decide that they need many times more clients to cover the risk of a single accident. So, because of the law of large numbers, if they developed a much larger pool of clients (say, 10,000 or 100,000), then their accident rate would likely to be much closer to the overall rate at which accidents really occur!

Incidentally, the law of large numbers is useful in understanding another phenomenon that some people may initially understand as rather spooky. Consider the following cases.

---

[15] Background note: Families may have all female children or all male children, but on average, total live births for the human species average around 1.05 boys for every girl.
http://vis.supstat.com/2013/04/law-of-large-numbers/.

Activity: Spooky events and probability

Bernard Beitman, a psychiatrist, reported that one day, he suddenly found himself unable to breathe for a moment. The next day, he discovered that his father had choked to death the previous day at right about the time he was unable to breathe for a moment.

A British soldier fighting in Italy was wounded in 1944. On the same day, at his family home in England, his wife later said to him, his two-year-old daughter had stopped playing for a moment and said "Daddy's been hurt!"

● *Are these stories proof that there are strange powers in the world, which are not and perhaps never will be explained by modern science?*[16]

These two examples, you may think, suggest that the world is stranger than we know. Well, that may be so. But a different way of thinking about it is that because of the huge number of people, and the even greater number of things that happen to them, some people are going to experience events that feel spooky, but which are just coincidences. If there is a large enough number of people having a large enough number of experiences, some of those experiences will be odd. But that doesn't mean that we should believe in the supernatural! Rather, while believing that some strange things will happen, we should assume that if we obtain a large enough data set, exceptions and unusual cases will cancel each other out, and that we will be able to obtain a fairly trustworthy set of information.

Of course, we must remember that the law of large numbers does not work for individual cases. We cannot use it to predict if a particular person will have a car accident or get a job after graduation. We can only use to predict roughly how many people will have a car accident per thousand drivers, or how many students in a group of 100 are likely not to graduate after four years at university.

Activity: Prediction in the human sciences

● *What do the following statements indicate about predictions in the human sciences?*
A) *"There is not the slightest possibility that nuclear energy will ever be obtainable." Albert Einstein, 1932.*
B) *"I think there is a world market for maybe five computers." Thomas Watson, chairman of IBM, 1943.*
C) *"The Beatles have no future in show business." Decca Records executive to manager Brian Epstein after an audition in 1962.*
D) *"Children just aren't interested in witches and wizards anymore." Publishing company executive to J.K. Rowling, 1996.*

---

[16] Both of these stories are from Bernard Beitman, *Connecting with coincidence*, HCI, 2016.

E) There's no chance that the iPhone is going to get any significant market share. No chance." Steve Ballmer, Microsoft CEO, 2007.

Trends and laws

In the human sciences, you may feel many predictions about the future are rather unreliable. Studies suggest that you would be right. Philip Tetlock concluded that predictions about world politics and economics by scholars, media figures, diplomats, and historians, were universally bad.[17] Economists don't predict recessions, political scientists didn't predict the victory of Trump, or the decision by a slight majority of British voters to leave the European Union. The demographer Malthus famously predicted that population increase would lead to a lack of resources, and mass human death, and that hasn't happened widely yet.

There are many reasons why human science predictions seem not to be very good. Among them, we can note that sometimes, these predictions are just based on the current situation or existing trends. Thus, the record company executive saying that the Beatles have no future, or the chairman of IBM saying that computers will not be popular, are basing their statements on the existing situation of the time. We could say that they are simply basing their statements on trends. Nothing like the Beatles had been popular in the past. Therefore, the executive expected that they would not be popular in the future. However, because the future was different to the past, the executive was completely wrong. Such trend-based predictions based on what happened in the past are not scientific. What has happened and what is happening is not necessarily a safe basis for predicting what will happen in the future. Induction-based knowledge, in short, is not necessarily a good guide to the future.

If you toss a coin and obtain heads nine times in a row, it doesn't mean that you have an increased chance of getting another head on the tenth toss. In order to make good predictions, we need to have reliable laws that state what should happen. Because of the huge number of factors that can affect each situation, however, such laws are quite difficult to achieve. Further, people may choose to go against expectations, if they know what is supposed to happen. Not only can predicting something make it come true (self-fulfilling predictions discussed above), but they can also stop something from coming true by changing our behaviour. If someone predicts that continued human activity will cause a rise in the planet's temperature

---

[17] Philip Tetlock, *Expert political judgment*, 2nd ed., Princeton University Press, 2017.

and that massive damage will result from that, then humans can decide to take action to prevent it from happening, for example.

A second problem with predictions in the human sciences is that we may be mistaken about the relationships between different phenomena. One famous case in economics concerns what is called the Phillips Curve, in which inflation, which is when prices increase and the purchasing power of money falls, was seen to be causally related to unemployment, based on an analysis of British economic data from the mid-19th century to the mid-20th century. To be exact, higher levels of employment were said to be correlated with higher levels of inflation. Based on this, governments were advised that accepting a certain level of inflation would help them to lower unemployment.

However, it turned out, especially in the 1970s, that many countries, including England and the United States, found that they experienced both high inflation and high unemployment at the same time. This indicated that the central idea behind the idea of the Phillips Curve was wrong. Increasingly, people became to understand that while there was a relationship between inflation and unemployment, it was not a simple one in which higher inflation caused lower unemployment. As has been seen in England and the US, high inflation and high unemployment can actually occur at the same time. In short, while two events had been seen to have a causal relationship, that idea was proven to be too simplistic. Just because two things happen together doesn't mean, in other words, that they are related, or that they have a causal relationship. A causal relationship means that one thing causes a change in another thing.

If two things occur together, then they may be correlated, or they may not. This means that it is possible that there is some causal connection between them, or it may be that the two things are not linked by anything more than coincidence or accident. The situation would need to be examined carefully. Secondly, if they are shown to be linked, then it would become necessary to consider how they are linked. Does one thing cause the other thing to occur, or is there some separate factor or factors that makes the two things occur at the same time? Because of the vast number of variables that affect human action, investigating these questions is not a simple task.

Activity: Correlations and causes

- *Consider the following combinations. Do you think they are accidental correlations (i.e., A and B are only connected by accident or coincidence, rather than any causality), causal correlations (A causes B, or B causes A), or correlations caused by some factor (C) that is not mentioned in the examples? What is your preferred hypothesis?*

A) *Smokers often are alcoholics.*
B) *Children who eat breakfast are more successful at school.*
C) *As countries get richer and better educated, birthrates drop.*
D) *Cigarettes smokers often get lung cancer (mouth, throat, tongue, stomach cancers etc. too).*
E) *Girls who watch a lot of soap operas and trendy dramas are more likely to have eating disorders.*
F) *Increasing sleep time from six hours a night to seven hours a night leads to a 10% increase in test scores.*
- *How would you test or verify your hypothesis, ideally? What makes it difficult to check your hypothesis in the real world?*

Complicating our ability to identify causal relationships is the fact that few events and actions in the human science have a single cause. Most things have relatively complex causation: they are the result of a range of factors that produced one result. If the range of factors had been a little different in some way, they may well have produced a very different result. The formation of a friendship, for example, is unlikely to be due to just one thing. The same goes for the decision to attend a particular university, to wear a particular set of clothes on a particular day, or to vote for a particular party or candidate. Obviously, the more complex a phenomenon becomes, the more factors must be considered in explaining why it happened.

Any explanation of large-scale phenomena such as the rise of imperialism or the spread of capitalism would need to pay attention to a huge number of factors. Obviously, because of this huge number of factors, it would be difficult to establish which factors matter, and how much. Any prediction about the future would also be likely to be unreliable, because it would need to include an immense number of factors, which are all in an interdependent relation with other factors. If you think about the future of human societies, for example, obviously the evolution of existing political, social, and economic arrangements (nation-states, transnational societies, global economy) must be considered. How these arrangements evolve will be related to environmental trends, as well as developments in scientific-technical knowledge. Artificial intelligence and transformations in the nature of work are also likely to be significant. But these interdependent factors are so complicated and so unpredictable that we cannot fully understand them at our current level of knowledge and understanding.

Activity: The complexity of causal factors

- *Take the case of a friendship or romantic relationship: how many factors were involved in making it happen? Is it easy to determine which factors were more important, and which were less important?*

Part 5. Explaining human behaviour

Reductionism and holism

Some approaches to studying the human sciences do not recognize that things are so complicated. One approach, called **reductionism**, says that everything that happens can be explained in terms of some simple basic principles.

- What is a human being? A collection of atoms including oxygen, carbon, hydrogen, nitrogen, calcium, phosphorus, potassium, sulphur, sodium, chlorine, magnesium, and other various trace elements.
- What is music? Waves of sound or vibration.
- Why did a person do something? Because a stimulus previous to that action aroused an impulse in our brain to do so.

Famously, the evolutionary biologist Richard Dawkins argued that much of human action can be explain either through genes—defined as the smallest units of functionally coded biological information—and natural selection, or by memes—defined as the smallest unit of cultural information—and natural selection.[18] Focusing on genes, for Dawkins, humans are carriers of genes. We may think that we live for ourselves, but actually, our bodies are for transmitting genes from one generation to the next. What we do is directed to making sure our genes are passed on. We cooperate with other family members, for example, to increase the chances of the family genes surviving into the future. In this way, the basic reason for all human action, in short, is that humans do things that lead to their genetic survival. Dawkins' ideas played a large role in the development of sociobiology, which explains social behaviour in terms of biological evolution. This type of reductionist natural science says that it is probably theoretically possible, although probably practically impossible, to obtain definite knowledge about human beings. This knowledge will be based on fundamental biology, chemistry, and physics.

Whether most people would accept an explanation of people's self-identity or sense of self that refers to external stimuli, chemicals in the body (biochemistry), brain wave patterns (neurophysics), and the operation of the nervous system (biology) is, however, quite doubtful. In fact, many scientists reject the reductionist approach. Dissecting a human being into organs and cells or reducing a human body

---

[18] Richard Dawkins, *The selfish gene*, Oxford University Press 1989.

to its basic chemicals can only tell us how it is made and what it is made of, not what it is like to live.

Those who take an approach known as **holism** argue that any attempt to understand human action needs to keep in mind the way in which not just genes and memes but also groups and institutions influence individuals, just as individuals themselves have an effect on memes, groups, and institutions. Individuals may seem to be whole beings on their own, but in fact, we exist within the context of larger societies of many people, and the qualities of the larger societies cannot be predicted or calculated from the properties of the individual people who make up that society. For example, studying individuals will not allow you to understand the whole of a language or a culture or a religion, but only the pieces that an individual is familiar with.[19]

In the human sciences, it is possible to see both reductionist and holist approaches. Microeconomics thinks about individuals as the basic actors of the economy, while macroeconomics tries to think about the economy as a whole, arguing that a grasp of individual actors doesn't allow you to understand the whole economy. Social anthropologists may try to get an understanding of a whole culture, and through that an understanding of the meaning of particular objects in that culture. Some psychologists and sociologists think that a person's psychology can be understood by looking at the groups that they belong to: people can be reduced to the qualities that are thought to be found in their nation, ethnicity, gender, class, etc.

Finally, there is a third alternative approach that can be taken, and that is called dialectical emergence. This approach takes the position that things are complicated and cannot be reduced to one property or process. Water, for example, is made up of oxygen and hydrogen, which are gases. Water is not the same as them, however. Water is a liquid with qualities that are not the same as those of oxygen or hydrogen alone. Applying this analogy to people, our minds may be based on neuro-chemical and neuro-physical processes, but it is not the same as them, if the mind is capable of consciousness, intention, comprehension, and control of the brain and body.

Activity: Cases for thinking about reductionism and holism

● *Try to explain how reductionists and holists would try to understand the following phenomena in different ways.*
A) *Why did a person do something bad?*
B) *Why is one baseball team good, and another team great?*

---

[19] This idea is associated with Emile Durkheim's 1895 essay, "What is a social fact", in *Rules of sociological method,* Free Press, 1982.

C)   Why does a human being feel bad when they make someone sad?
D)   Why is the same class different at different times and with different teachers?

Understanding in the human sciences

In the natural sciences, the main aim is to understand simple cause and effect. Why apples fall to the ground, or why ageing occurs, or why the combination of certain chemicals leads to a particular reaction and so forth may be typical cases. What the natural sciences typically do not focus on is the meaning or purpose for people of particular actions and things.

We might think about this difference by looking at the case of Alfred Nobel. In a case of massively successful branding, Nobel is famous today mainly for having his name on a set of prestigious prizes in the humanities as well as social and natural science. However, he originally became rich by developing the explosive known as dynamite, as well as by transforming the iron and steel company Bofors into a major weapons manufacturer operating 90 factories. Nobel's scientific career was in natural science, mainly chemistry, and he was very successful in working out how to make things explode with great force and accuracy, as well as in making weapons. But a popular explanation for his establishment of the Nobel Foundation says that he became aware that he was known primarily as a "merchant of death". It was literally true, of course: his inventions and products were for killing more people more efficiently. However, Nobel hated the idea that he would be remembered for this and decided to set up the Nobel Foundation and prizes to improve his reputation. Without knowing about Nobel's concern with the perceived meaning of what he did in other people's eyes, we cannot understand his actions. How people understand things, in short, explains why they do things, and the natural sciences do not tell us about these understandings.

Natural science doesn't deal with this type of issue because its objects— atoms, molecules, rocks, chemicals, DNA, genes and so on—are not self-aware. They don't do things because of their beliefs and understandings and perception of the attitudes of others. But such things are very important for humans and so must be in the human sciences. Natural science may explain how things happen, but human sciences focus on why things happen in terms of meaningfulness to human actors.

The significance of this can be seen if you imagine the case of aliens who come to earth and watch traffic lights. When traffic lights turn red, cars tend to stop. When they turn green, cars tend to go. For an alien, one obvious hypothesis would be that red lights cause cars to stop, and green lights cause cars to go. Of course, this would be wrong. What actually happens is that the meaning of red lights for humans is "stop", and the meaning of green lights for humans is "go". What seems to happen, when viewed from an external viewpoint, is likely to be very different to what is happening when viewed from the point of view of the people who are actually involved.

Consider something like having sex. Reductionists may focus on biological impulses to reproduce, or pleasurable impulses in the brain and so forth. Holists may like to focus on the wider social context in which individuals engage in sexual activity. However, it is surely important to understand sexual activity from the point of view of the people engaging in it: How do they understand what they are doing? What kinds of meanings do they perceive that activity to have? Max Weber said that social practices need to be understood from the point of view of the actors involved. This is sometimes called *Verstehen*, from the German word for understanding, but it is fundamentally the same as the sociological perspective known as symbolic interactionism.[20] This means that if we want to understand someone's actions, we need to know what meanings the actors saw in their actions. Because different actors act from different motivations and with different meanings in mind, it is obvious that universal laws will be rare in the human sciences.

Activity: Meanings and actions

- *Use your imagination to suggest as many possible meanings that the following actions could have as possible.*
A) *Singing in a karaoke room.*
B) *Drinking alcohol.*
C) *Getting out a gun.*
D) *Waving your hand at someone.*
E) *Signing your name.*

Unintended consequences

We should add that sometimes, people do things without knowing quite what they do. Or, to be more accurate, people do things, but without awareness of the wider consequences of what they do. The Verstehen approach is not able to handle these kinds of phenomena. Some examples of important cases of unintended consequences include the following.

- Adam Smith wrote in *The Wealth of Nations* (1776) about how people tried to maximize their own benefits from their economic behavior. As a result, there was a tendency for people to specialize in the economic activities that they were best at. To obtain the things they were not so good at making, people traded what

---

[20] Joseph Heath, "Methodological Individualism", in Edward N. Zalta, ed., *The Stanford Encyclopedia of Philosophy* (Spring 2015 Edition), URL = <https://plato.stanford.edu/archives/spr2015/entries/methodological-individualism/>.

they made for what others made. This system of individuals trying to make the best outcome for themselves ended up creating a capitalist world economy. Obviously, no single individual was thinking about the creation of a capitalist world economy when trying to achieve the most profit possible.

● Max Weber provided a similar kind of example regarding capitalism, with his explanation focusing on the Protestant religion (*The Protestant Ethic and the Spirit of Capitalism*, 1904-1905). Protestants believed in predestination, or the idea that their god had chosen some people to succeed and live good lives, and that others were damned from the beginning. The problem was, of course, how to know which group an individual was in. Many believers tried to find proof that God approved of them, or that they were destined for a good life and to go to heaven. One sign of God's blessing, they decided, was being wealthy. In response to this religious belief, many Protestants stressed the importance of hard work and making a profit. Further, once they made a profit, they didn't spend it on luxuries or give it away to the poor. Rather, they reinvested it, in technological improvements and in new ventures, to make more money. As Protestants acted to try and reassure themselves that they were going to heaven, they helped to create the capitalist world economy. Of course, Weber's explanation was about how over time, the religious aspect declined, and people started to engage in economic activity in order simply to become wealthy, rather than in order to be wealthy so that they could feel sure that God approved of them. But the effect is still the same: People's attempts to become wealthy have unintended consequences such as the globalization of capital, world trade, consumerism, environmental destruction, and so forth.

● The tension between the two Koreas has led to the creation of a demilitarized zone between the two. This has had the effect of creating a large nature zone with bountiful wildlife, which was not at all the intended effect!

These kinds of unintended effects of people's actions are also of interest to the human sciences, and they cannot be grasped from looking just at the meanings of events as understood by the participants of those events. An external or outside viewpoint is necessary in these cases.

The limits of economic rationality

A famous case of unintended consequences that gives us a sense of how complicated the human sciences are is outlined by Samuel Bowles.[21] So many parents were coming late to pick up their children that six Israeli day-care centres introduced a penalty for late pick-ups. This was an idea taken from economics: to make people stop doing something, make it costlier for them to do it, in this case by charging them more money. However, this didn't work as planned. Twice as many parents came late as before. Basically, the original hypothesis—that parents were late because there was no penalty for late pick-ups—proved to be wrong. Far from solving the problem, introducing a penalty made it worse. Reducing the problem to a

---

[21] Samuel Bowles, *The Moral Economy*, Yale University Press, 2016.

question of economic rationality and money proved to be an unsatisfactory explanation.

Therefore, a new hypothesis became necessary. One suggestion was that before, even though they were often late, parents felt that they shouldn't be late because they were taking up day-care workers' private time. But now that they were being charged money, this sense of guilt was no longer a problem. Parents felt that they had lost their obligation to be considerate to workers since there was a fee for being late. The economic cost of being late—an extra fee—replaced the moral cost of being late—feeling bad about being late and inconveniencing the workers. Clearly, however, the bigger issue was that in the wider contexts of their economic and social lives, parents were so busy that it was difficult for them to meet their obligation to the day-care centre to pick up their children on time. Solving this problem would require either the day-care centre extending child-care hours, either modifying people's working situations, as well as traffic conditions, and so on. In short, a holist explanation that looked not just at economic rationality, but also moral concerns, parents' understandings, the position of work in society and so on, seems to provide a better but rather more complicated explanation in this case.

The economist Dani Rodrik uses a similar logic to think about the case of carbon emissions control.[22] Are people's actions more affected by moral feelings than economic motivations? In other words, if we charge more for high emissions cars with large inefficient engines, as well as for airplane travel (which is the most energy-inefficient form of travel), then won't people simply think that this allows them to keep on emitting more? Does the day-care example show that campaigns to educate the public by appealing to a moral duty to reduce our emissions may be more successful than a program to make people and companies pay for the amount of emissions they are responsible for?

Clearly, simple cause and effect do not explain what people do all of the time. It may be true that higher costs will change people's behaviour. But there are different types of costs, both moral and financial, and different people will understand those different costs in different ways. Further, people today are more and more aware of how others (governments, advertising agencies, teachers, parents, etc.) try to influence them. How will people who are increasingly aware of the expectations of others act? We can't really say. Because of this complexity, the human sciences seem to provide a relatively uncertain basis for understanding human social, economic, and political life.

---

[22] Dani Rodrik, *Economics rules*, W.W. Norton 2015.

The human sciences in review

Overall, the human sciences have fewer absolute laws and make less accurate predictions that the natural sciences, but this is not because they are weaker or less scientific. Rather, it is because the human sciences are much more complicated. Dealing with human action requires an understanding of human thinking, but human thinking is not accessible to us directly. Indirect access is possible, using surveys and questionnaires, but such questions and answers may contain various biases. Observation is also possible but has the problem that observation may change people's behaviour. Further, the data that is obtained from such methods needs to be interpreted, and such interpretation may be affected by bias as well.

Most researchers, while aware of the need to keep an open and critical mind, are likely to have preferred positions, theories that they don't agree with, and so forth. In short, they are likely to have an unconscious tendency towards confirmation bias and will pay more attention to ideas that fit with their beliefs than to ideas that contradict their beliefs. In order not to fall victim to bias linked to our own preferences, it is important to always actively look for examples and data that goes against what we believe. Of course, in the sciences more generally, as scientists check and re-check each other's results, the level of reliability should improve.

Making things even more complicated is the fact that social phenomena are quite hard to measure, and even small differences in the way that scientists do their research may lead to large differences between them. For example, ideas and meanings are important in the human sciences, but how to understand them is a big problem. This is because different people are likely to understand things in different ways. Quantitative data such as statistics, consumer information, and so forth provides new ways to measure things. However, qualitative surveys looking in more depth at people's understandings of their own lives are also important. Robert Murphy, for example, wrote a personal anthropological narrative about how he experienced losing the ability to move his arms and legs due to a spinal problem, and how his understanding of his body and sickness and medical treatment evolved.[23] This kind of deep understanding of what people think and feel is not available to us through quantitative studies, at least not at the current time.

Based on observation and measurement, the scientific process should lead to hypotheses about what the world is like. But in the human sciences, of course, predictions can become self-fulfilling prophecies, or lead people to do the opposite of what is predicted. Since predictions can have such a large effect on people,

---

[23]Robert Murphy, *The body silent*, Henry Holt and Company, 1987.

hypothesis testing would require a double process, one to see if the hypothesis affects the behaviour, and another to see if the hypothesis itself is supported. In order to investigate both of these questions, experiments or tests in controlled conditions would ideally be conducted. However, unlike with natural science experiments, it is difficult to control for all factors in the human sciences. Isolating subjects from the rest of society and accounting for the effects of class, education, race and ethnicity, sexual orientation, personal beliefs, and so forth is incredibly difficult. Further, such experiments also are likely to involve ethical issues of whether it is permissible to isolate some people, and to make them engage in certain types of actions.

Because of these various issues, then, the human sciences tend to come up with laws that are limited in scope, and which have relatively low predictive power. We are better at finding trends than universal laws, and the laws that we do have are more probabilistic than definite.

Finally, it is important to add that there is another huge difference between the human and natural sciences, which concerns value judgments, or issues such as good and bad, justice and unfairness. While an ethically neutral understanding of how the body works, or gravity, may be possible, it is not clear that this can be done in the case of at least some human matters. One example concerns how one might describe Nazi Germany. In order to describe it in ethically neutral language, one might say that it was "a society that chose to dominate one sector of its population in the aim of restoring national confidence". But such a form of description seems undesirable. Perhaps value neutrality is not possible in the human sciences in the same way that it is in the natural sciences.

Chapter 3 Determinism and freedom

Noah McCormack

Part 1. Determinism in the human sciences

This third brief chapter considers the debate over determinism and human freedom. We all want to be free (apparently), but what it means to be free, and what we can actually be free from, are issues that most of us have not thought about in too much detail. Here, we offer a brief introduction to current debates over how much we are determined by our genes and society, and whether we can do anything about this level of freedom, and whether we should care!

The effects of genes, and of society and family

What makes you uniquely you? How different would you be if you had grown up in a different family in a different place? How much of you is the result of your interactions with the world after birth, and how much is due to the genes you got from your parents? The answers to these questions are incredibly complex.

The genes we get or inherit make us who we are. The experiences that we have in society also make us who we are. Genetics and life experience both are of roughly equal importance. But sorting out their relative impact is very difficult.[24] Consider the following cases:

Activity: Social and genetic influences on humans

- **Correlation: Parents and children resemble each other, for example, in being talkative.** *What are the possible explanations for this similarity? At a minimum, the five hypotheses below need to be addressed.*
A) It might be because they share genetic information: the children inherited talkative genes from their parents.
B) It might be because of social experiences (a) living with talkative parents made the children talkative.
C) It might be because of social experiences (b) having talkative children made the parents talkative.
D) The talkativeness of parents and children might have different causes, for example, one parent is genetically talkative, the other became talkative because

---

[24] The following discussion is adapted from Steven Pinker, *The blank slate. The modern denial of human nature*, Penguin, 2002, especially chapter 19.

they enjoy communicating with co-workers, one child inherited talkative genes, and another child became talkative by interacting with talkative friends.

E) A, B, C and D are all true.

● *Does any possibility seem more likely to you than the others? How could you investigate the relative truth of these possibilities?*

Actually, you might think that genetic influences and family environment should be about of equal importance. But Pinker says, based on studies of identical and non-identical twins as well as of adopted children that try to clarify the relative importance of these influences, that the effects of family environment appear in fact to be rather small. He makes three observations based on a consideration of a wide range of studies

● Adult brothers and sisters are equally similar, whether they grew up together or apart.

● Adoptive siblings who grew up in the same family are no more similar than two people chosen at random in the street.

● Identical twins are no more similar than you would expect from the effects of their shared genes.

Activity: family effects and genetic effects

● *What logical conclusions concerning the effects of family environment can be drawn from this set of observations?*

Activity: Shared family characteristics

Category	Specific issues / topics	The people who raised you	
		Guardian 1	Guardian 2
Ideas about politics	Constitutional change		
	Preferred political party		
	Nuclear energy / renewables		
Ideas about society	Pro / anti- immigration		
	Pro / anti- tourism		
	Pro / anti- minority sexuality		
	Preferred type of marriage partner		
Ideas about economy	Free trade / protectionism		
	Desirable companies / industries		
	Privatization / state enterprises		
Personality traits	Sense of humour		
	Work / study ethic		
	Preferred entertainments		

Taking yourself as the baseline, write down an M for "Match", D for "Different", or U for "Unknown".

● *What do the results suggest about the relationship between you and the people who raised you? Did they determine or decide who you are and what you are like? Do you think you had a choice in how you became who you are, or not?*

What about now? Do you have more choice now? If you compare yourself to your siblings (if you have any), what level of similarity do you think exists?

Does it seem possible to say that the way we are is mainly the result of our own free and conscious choices? Or does it seem more likely, instead, that our genes combined with the conditions in which we grow up and the people with whom we interact and the experiences that we have determine who we are? If so, maybe it becomes possible to say that life makes us who we are; it looks quite hard to say that we make ourselves. And if so, perhaps we are not as in control of our own lives as we like to think. At the very least, we should think about how free we really are to decide who we are and how we will live.

The question of whether we are free to decide who we are and how we will live is significant in several ways. For one thing, the fact that we praise and criticize people for what they do assumes that people are free to choose what they do. If we are free to choose what we do, then it is reasonable to praise people who choose to do things that we think are good, and to criticize people who choose to do things that we disapprove of. If people's acts are involuntary or predetermined, if people were not free to choose, then it wouldn't make sense to praise someone's good acts or to criticize someone's bad acts. In line with this idea, we do not think people who are mentally insane are responsible for their actions. We figure that they cannot freely choose what they do and are unfree in their actions. But do most people really act in a free and conscious way most of the time?

Activity: Free decisions

- *What kinds of things do you think that people decide freely? How free do you think they are in making those "free" decisions? What kinds of factors need to be considered in answering these two questions?*

Two kinds of free will

Our world values freedom very highly. However, what we mean by this term is not completely obvious. Commonly, we use it to refer to "surface freedoms." If we are able to choose what we eat and drink and wear, select our friends and romantic partners, vote for political representatives, and so on, without anyone or anything trying to stop us or control us, then we enjoy this kind of surface freedom.

On the other hand, we would not be free, in this sense of the term, if we were brainwashed to want something, or if we were addicted to something, because in those cases, we would be "forced" to have that desire. Similarly, if you are given a choice of "your money or your life" by an armed robber, then this is not really a choice either. You are being forced to hand over your money, because hopefully you value your money much less than you value your life. If we use this shallow meaning of freedom, then many of us enjoy a high level of freedom every day.[25]

Philosophers think, however, that this kind of freedom is quite shallow. The much more interesting question is, "Can we have freedom over the things that we want?" Because while we can enjoy surface freedom to do what we want, if we are not free to choose what we want, then that freedom is really not free! Consider, for example, the kinds of clothes that you want to wear, or the movies that you want to watch, or the music that you want to listen to. It is highly likely that your desires, which you may feel are "free", have been manipulated or influenced by advertising and marketing companies, as well as by your friends and peers, the people you see around you in public, and so forth. In this sense, even when you feel like you are free, you may not really be acting freely—you're just unaware of how others are making you want to do what you want to do. Because you don't control what you want, you can have surface freedom to do what you want (Freedom 1), but you don't have deeper freedom to decide what you want (Freedom 2). Of course, many scholars will then say that Freedom 2 is an illusion: we cannot have desires free of our genetics and free of the environment in which we grew up! We cannot cause ourselves, free of the outside world.

The position that people don't really make free decisions is known as **determinism**. The basic argument of determinism is that everything that happens, including human actions and speech, has a cause. Without that cause, the decision or action would not have happened. That cause, which might be a combination of different factors or a single factor, determined what would happen next. If so, then even if we think we make decisions freely, our actual decisions are in fact already decided—even though we may not be aware of this.

Activity: Clothing choice

● *What are you wearing today? Why did you choose that? Was it a free decision— in other words, could you have chosen something else? But you didn't! Why not? Is it because your decision was already decided?*

Free will and responsibility

This issue connects to the issue of responsibility mentioned earlier. If we only have Freedom 1, this may have important implications for what we think about the responsibility of individuals for their actions. Imagine that someone commits a brutal murder of someone that you know, and you attend the trial full of anger towards the

---

[25] Robert Kane, *A contemporary introduction to free will*, Oxford University Press, 2005.

killer. But, during the trial, it emerges that the killer was not only neglected but also severely abused, physically and sexually, from elementary school until the end of junior high school. From junior high school, the killer lived homeless on the streets, surviving in a brutal and savage society of gangsters, criminals, and drug addicts. Learning this, perhaps your anger shifts. It may be that you start to feel that it is not just the killer, but also the people who raised the killer, those who interacted with the killer, as well as the society that allowed a child to grow up in such deprivation and violence, who all share the blame. At this point, the question may start to arise of whether the young killer is ultimately and solely responsible for the killing.

More broadly, how responsible can we be for the way in which others raise us, and for the people that we become? Do those influences determine who we became 100%, or is there some part that we decided, freely in the sense of Freedom 2, and which we are therefore responsible for? Did the killer become a killer because of the circumstances in which the killer grew up, and the genes that they received, or did the killer become a killer of their own free will?

These kinds of questions begin to arise, says Kane, when people reach a high level of self-consciousness, and start to suspect that what they do is determined or brought about by factors that they themselves cannot control. People start to wonder about why they do the things they do, and why they have the ideas they have.[26]

Activity: The Why game

- *In groups of three, play the "why" game, with two people asking a third why she or he likes a particular idol group / movie / TV program. Each answer should be followed up with the question why, until the responder cannot answer any further. Does this process suggest something about the likelihood of determinism being an important force in our lives?*

At an intuitive level, it may seem obvious that everything that happens has a prior cause, or something that made it happen. Every time we do or say something, it is caused by something that happened earlier, and so on. In theory, with unlimited access to data, it should be possible to answer major questions such as how the universe came to exist, as well as minor questions such as why your parents got together and created you, and why you are reading these sentences. Do these ideas suggest that we have no free will, and that unlimited data and computing power would allow us to predict not only everything that has happened, but also everything that will happen?

---

[26] Kane, *op. cit.*

People who want to believe in free will disagree and say that people are able to gain knowledge about the factors that influence them, and can choose to obey those influences, or to go against them. For example, the values you learn from the people who raise you are likely to make you better at certain types of jobs and occupations. But you are also able to become aware of how you have been influenced. If you become aware of the influences that have affected you, then you can make a conscious choice about whether to follow the values you were raised with, or not. Such a decision would still be strongly influenced by your experiences in life. But it would seem, at the very least, that we would feel we were making a free and conscious choice.

However, some rather controversial experiments in physiology suggest that this is not necessarily true. In the 1980s, Benjamin Libet showed that electrical activity occurs in the brain (In the figure below, RP) before we become aware that we're going to do something (W), and then we do it (T). In other words, our brains apparently decide to do something, and then we become consciously aware of that decision immediately afterwards. If this is true for all of our actions, we cannot have free will to decide what to do—our brains automatically or subconsciously decide things—then our brains tell us about it, and we think we are making the decision freely.

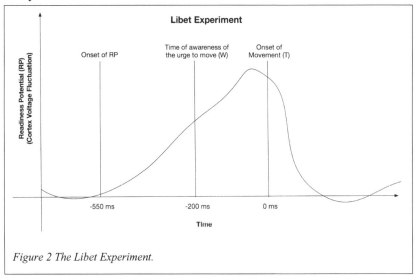

Figure 2 The Libet Experiment.

As knowledge about neuroscience increases, it seems that more and more people accused of criminal actions are using determinist arguments to explain and partially justify their actions. It has also been shown, in experiments by Kathleen Vohs and Jonathan Schooler, that people who are taught that free will is an illusion and that determinism is powerful are more likely to cheat and steal. The reason seems to be that when people don't think they are free, they feel that they are less responsible for what they do, and act less morally. They reason that even if they do something bad, people will say their bad act was already determined. That is, it wasn't their conscious or deliberate choice. Other experiments by Roy Baumeister suggest that belief in the idea that free will is an illusion makes people less likely to give money to poor people or lend people their cell phone or to help classmates. It even makes people feel less happy, lessening people's confidence in the belief that their lives have meaning. Also, the loss of belief in free will means that people cannot be expected to be praised for moral actions, and so we lose a powerful force that makes people do good as well. Belief in determinism and the idea that free will is an illusion seems to have strong negative effects on society and on individuals.[27]

We face a kind of dilemma. Belief in free will seems to be useful and good. But whether we have much free will seems doubtful. Sam Harris argues that we should recognize that people who do the worst things—mass murderers, torturers, and so on—are unlucky people who didn't choose their own genes, parents, and brains, even though these factors are major causes of what they do.[28] To an important degree, what they did is not their responsibility; they are more like natural disasters, he argues, than deliberately or consciously bad people. Thus society, rather than emotionally taking revenge on such people or harshly punishing them, should more rationally consider ways to rehabilitate them. If that seems impossible, it should take steps to protect society and reduce the risk of re-offending, possibly by neurochemical treatments of psychopathologies. Overcoming our belief in free will would also let us overcome fear and resentment and so on as well, Harris argues, because we would start to see the way other people are as being beyond their control, as well as beyond our control.

Harris makes the important point that people who are told free will is an illusion are more likely to do immoral action because they misunderstand what determinism means. Fatalism is the belief that what we do and decide doesn't really matter because everything is already decided. This position can lead people to think that nothing they do really matters. But determinism is not the same as fatalism. It just says that what we do is part of long chain of cause and effect that cannot be broken. It doesn't say that what we choose to do doesn't matter. If we think that determinism is fatalism, then we may be more likely to do bad things. But a different conception of determinism may help people to be better. We may not fully control the choices that we make, but we can still make choices that make a difference in the world. Namely, if we teach people that they should look for many possible courses of

---

[27] Roy F. Baumeister, Alfred R. Mele, Kathleen D. Vohs, *Free will and consciousness—How might they work?* Oxford University Press, 2010.
[28] Sam Harris, *Free will*, The Free Press, 2012.

action, and that they should try to choose good options and stock to them, we are likely to produce better results.

Activity: Changing yourself using free will

A)   Can you decide to study more, or less?
B)   Is being mean or being kind something that is fixed for life?
C)   Can you decide to start being a love rat, or to stop being a love rat?
D)   Is it possible to start to like something you hate, just because you decided to?
E)   Can you decide to get interested in people you find boring?
F)   Can you decide to work hard if you're lazy?
G)   Can you decide to show concern for others if you're selfish?

Many of the things we do are routine. These decisions we don't think about so much, and we do them almost automatically, without thinking. We decide what to wear, what to eat, what to watch, and so forth with little conscious thought. Sometimes, we think about things a little more. If your lover proposes marriage, or if a company offers you a job, then you're likely to think about it a little bit. You may examine your options, and weigh up the pros and the cons. But you may not know exactly how you made a decision. No doubt, whatever you choose, you're likely to feel it was your decision. But how you chose may be, ultimately, mysterious.

Activity: Choosing a job

● *If you are offered a job by several different companies, you'll need to choose one from among them (or, you could refuse all of them). In making these decisions, are you choosing freely? Could you choose any of them?*
● *Determinism says that because of your genetics and upbringing, you can only choose the possibility that you actually choose, and the others look like possibilities, but actually are not. What do you think?*

Activity: Unfree actions and consciousness

● *Spinoza long ago said that our sense of being free comes from the fact that we are conscious of our actions, but ignorant of the causes. Do you agree?*

Everyday freedom may be seen as just doing what you want, without being forced to do something, or as having a choice between several different options. But doing what you want can also be unfree if you are addicted to something. The difference between addiction, in which people are unfree to choose, and desire, in which people choose to want something somewhat freely, is not absolute, but just of degree. Having a choice may be important for freedom, although it may be that we cannot choose other than what we choose…

To end, it is perhaps useful to return to a perspective from psychology. At the beginning of this section on free will, we noted that half of who we are (personality, intelligence, behaviour) appears to be genetically determined. The other half comes from "something" in the environment. But because siblings who grow up together in the same shared family environment show no similarities beyond those that are genetically determined, we should look elsewhere to identify the nature of that "something" in the environment.

According to Judith Harris[29], the answer is that children live in societies of children: the other children that a child interacts with have a much greater influence on tastes, interests, values, and skills than the parents do. Some children steal motorbikes and smoke cigarettes to achieve status among their peers. Other children try to get ultra-high grades on tests to achieve status among their peers. The language children use, the fashion and entertainment they consume, the dreams they have, come from other children, not parents. Parents may provide skills and knowledge, but values and norms tend to come from peers.

Does this explain a child's personality too? Do children with different genetically determined personalities get sorted into different peer groups? Well, given than identical twins with the same friends are only 50% similar, this doesn't seem to be the case. For Judith Harris, this is explained by the fact that within peer groups, children have different roles—leaders, jokers, peacemakers, loose cannons—and what each child becomes depends on what roles are available, what the child is like, and "chance". "Chance" or "luck", whether good or bad, may in fact be a major factor in deciding how we and our lives turn out.

Activity: random chance

A)   Make a list of at least five things you almost did but didn't.
B)   Then make a list of at least five things you did, but almost didn't.
●   Probably, there is a considerable amount of random chance in making you turn out as you are. You could easily have become someone rather different!

If the non-genetic part of our personality is the outcome of a kind of "roulette", we are substantially genetically determined, and also substantially the results of "fate", which we can define as uncontrollable fortune, and not "free will". In the end, whether we have free will may not really be the right question. What we become, in terms of personality and character and values, is largely beyond our control. This has two important implications. One is that parents are not responsible for how their children turn out—they can't make their children be how they want them to be; fate is far more important. Another clear implication is that even if our lives are not turning out the way that we want, we cannot blame our parents for this. We all share a responsibility, on the other hand, for maintaining the health of the

---

[29] Judith Harris, *The nurture assumption: why children turn out the way they do*, The Free Press, 1998, rev. ed. 2009.

communities and cultures in which peer groups exist, and in which people can develop and live while respecting each other's dignity.

Chapter 4 The Historical Sciences

Patrick Strefford

Part 1. Individual and social pasts

What would you do if you totally lost your memory? Imagine that one day you wake up, and you have no memory of anything that has happened to you. You wouldn't know who you are. You wouldn't know where you are. It sounds like quite a scary situation to be in.

Let's take another example. When meeting someone for the first time, what do we often ask? Well, we ask their name, we ask about their job or their studies, we ask about their hobbies and interests. Frequently, we also ask where they are from. Why? We want to learn about them, and a key part of this is learning about their past.

Why is the past—our own, and other peoples—so important? Well, in an important sense, our past is who we are. A person's biography gives details about the process of how each individual came into being. We are made by our experiences: our education, our families, our society, culture. The question "Who am I?" is basically asking "How was I made?", or "How did I become like this?" Therefore, if we lost our memories of our experiences, we would no longer be the people we are. Losing our pasts, we would have lost our identities. We would no longer know ourselves—we wouldn't know how to act or what to do.

Understanding other people's pasts, in short, is a way to understand people. If you know your past, or other people's pasts, then you can better understand yourself and others. And if you understand yourself and other people better, you can predict your actions and reactions, as well as those of others. In short, knowledge about personal pasts provides us with a kind of power that helps us to operate in the world. The academic discipline of history, we shall suggest, can help to empower us in similar ways.

In this chapter we will look at history in a number of different ways. First, we will answer the question, what is history? Then, we will investigate the very important reasons why we must study history. Thirdly, we will look at how we study history. This will include sections on evidence and potential biases, as well as different theories of history.

Activity: Biography and self-re-construction

- *Bring two photos of yourself to class. One should be quite recent, and one from early childhood.*
A) *Today, to what extent are you (a) the same person, and (b) a different person, from the "you" who appears in the two photos? What events in your autobiography caused you to change?*
B) *Look at the two photos that another student has brought to class. Imagine that person has lost their memory completely, and that these photos are the only existing traces of that person's past. What kinds of information or clues can you find in them about who they used to be?*

What is History?

Significance

History is 'the study of the past'. But, does it deal with all of the past, or just part of the past? Well, of course, we do not study *all* of the past, nor do we know about *all* of the past. Therefore, we should say that history is 'part of the past', or 'the study of part of the past'. So, which parts do we study? Which parts do we know? Well, we study *significant* parts of the past. History deals with those events in the past that are seen to be important from a later perspective. This perspective changes through time.

In societies dominated by men, history tended to focus on areas of human life that were important for men, such as war and government. But with the rise in women's power from especially the 1960s onwards, views on what is significant have changed. Topics such as domestic labor, gender relations, and reproduction are considered to be as significant as war, for example, and women's history has become a very broad and well-established field.

The same can be said for various ethnic, racial, and sexual minorities. Their pasts were once seen to have little historical significance, but as minorities' power increased through the processes of decolonization, the so-called human rights revolution after the second world war, and grassroots mobilization, their pasts became seen to be widely significant, and are being written into history. Thus, we could say, as societies change, so too does what is seen as significant, and as a result, the content of history changes too.

General criteria for judging whether an event is significant or not would include the numbers of people involved, and how much they are affected. For example, a disease that affects millions of people is more likely to be considered of historical importance than a disease that only affects several people. But in addition to the number of people affected, the degree to which they are affected will also be important. Millions of people catching a cold and feeling a bit sick for a few days will not be considered to be significant, but 35 million people dying as a result of the AIDS virus will be considered significant.

One interesting problem with significance is that things that may not seem important when they occur can become significant later, and vice versa. The birth of a baby to a poor couple in a horse shed somewhere in today's Palestine over 2000 years ago probably didn't seem important to anyone but the baby's parents. However, the subsequent development of an organized world religion centred on Jesus Christ means that his birth is considered historically significant today.

The opposite can also be true: things can appear to be very important as they happen but lose their significance over time. At the moment, the so-called War on Terror led by the United States may seem rather important. But over the next thousand years, this evaluation may change. If there is an alien invasion or massive suffering related to environmental catastrophe during this time, then it is quite possible that the significance of this war will be greatly reduced. In the long term, the historical significance of any event will depend on how things turn out later, and what role that event is seen to have played in those later developments.

We can say, therefore, that history involves studying what we think is significant about the past. It tries to describe what happened, and to explain why it happened, and therefore, to make it clear why things have turned out as they are. In this sense, it is somewhat like autobiography or biography, which try to explain a person's character and personality by examining their past experiences.

Evidence

Secondly, the academic discipline of history is based on evidence. Human history before writing developed was once called pre-history, and history was considered to involve the study of written evidence from the past. However, today, the study of history can involve oral sources, like tape recordings of music or interviews with older people about what life was like in their youth, as well as poems, sculptures and artwork, everyday items including clothes and buildings, personal records such as diaries and letters, and so on.

In short, history involves analysing various different types of evidence from the past that still exist today. Obviously, we find more of some types of evidence than others. For example, it is much easier to study more powerful groups and people, as well as more recent periods, simply because there is much more evidence available about them. On the other hand, there is not so much evidence remaining about very ancient times, and less powerful people and groups. Because of this problem of evidence availability, historical studies must constantly deal with the problem of bias.

Activity: Measures of significance

Make a list of the three most significant events:		Why do you think they are significant?	What kinds of evidence do you have access to about these events?
In your life so far	*1)* *2)* *3)*		
In Japan during your lifetime	*1)* *2)* *3)*		
In the world during your lifetime	*1)* *2)* *3)*		

The functions of history

Do we really need to understand history? How is it important for us? Well, obviously, if you are studying International Relations, then history is essential knowledge. Indeed, if you are studying any social science or humanities field, then history is an important part of your study. But, how about the rest of us? Why do we need to study "yesterday's news"?

History may not appear to be immediately useful in an economic or financial sense. It's unlikely that by studying history, you will learn how to make goods, provide services, or make money. But from a human science point of view, there are a number of very important reasons for studying history:

1. We know that personal history gives us our individual identity. In the same way, collective (group) histories give us collective (group) identity. National history is essential for national identity, and transnational or global history will be necessary for any emerging cosmopolitan identity set at the global or world level.

2. Knowledge of history is a defense against propaganda and fake news. If we have knowledge of history, then we will have more resistance to the historical lies and misinformation that leaders and other powerful figures sometimes try to claim.
3. Understanding human history helps us to understand just how diverse humans are. We can learn how humans behave in different situations, at different times.
4. We cannot understand "today's news" without understanding "yesterday's news". Our present reality was made by the events of the past. If we do not understand how those events made our reality, then we cannot understand the world around us.

History and group identity

"A country without a history is like a person without a memory"

Any group of people has customs, traditions, norms and values that are particular to that group. All of these things make up the collective or shared identity of the members of that group. If we want to interact with that group, we need to understand those things, and to do this, it is necessary to study how these customs, traditions and norms came to be used. Basically, we must study the history of these things.

Of course, we should say that people have many different identities. We could say, indeed, that people have layers of identities. We all have an individual identity, but then connected to this is the identity we have from being members of different groups. Identity is the connection between the individual and the group. Some connections are stronger and some are weaker.

We could say that groups build identities over time, and so history is the process of building group identity. In this way, any group will try to preserve its history because of this connection to identity. When you start working at a company after you graduate, one of the first things the company will do is tell the history of the company. Schools and university also present their history to students because it is connected to the identity of the school or university. Towns and cities will have monuments and museums that preserve and present the history of the place. The purpose of all of these attempts is to build a sense of collective identity—of belonging together to a company, a school or university, a town or city—based on a shared history.

Possibly the most important (and most problematic) example of this is the history of nations. In political philosophy, the term "nation" usually refers to a group of people who claim the right to govern themselves (e.g., Renan, Weber). Nationalists claim that national identity should be one of our strongest identities.

Media and political discourse during events such as the Olympics or the World Cup show that this idea is very powerful. How does such a group form?

Different to the relatively naturally occurring feeling of belonging to a small-scale community like a family or a village, the feeling of belonging to a nation—an "imagined community" as Benedict Anderson[30] put it—comes from nation-states. More precisely, nation-states develop and teach a national history curriculum to all children, they establish museums and galleries devoted to the nation's history, and to its art, they have research institutions that study the nation's origins and development, and so forth. They create a history centred on what is significant *from the perspective of national development*. Other possibilities—events and trends that did not connect with national development—are excluded from their history. In this way, nations create history that strengthens national identity.

There are two important points to take from this discussion. One is that promoting the feeling that people have a shared past is a very powerful way to get people to feel a sense of togetherness and form a strong united group. Another is that companies and educational institutions and states try to use this knowledge, to make people into united groups that will be useful *for* those companies and educational institutions and states. To live as active subjects of our own lives, it is good to be aware of this ambiguous or double-edged function of history.

History and power

George Orwell, the author of *1984* and *Animal Farm* referred to this double-edged nature of history when he said, "Who controls the past controls the future, who controls the present controls the past". Basically, he meant that history is made by those who have the power to decide what is significant for everyone. What those people choose as history affects how people understand their situation and their identity, and so it affects their actions too. By having the power to control the contents of history today, the powerful have the power to shape what happens tomorrow. This quotation suggests to us, in short, why many governments make considerable efforts to influence their nations' history, and why narratives about a nation's history are so often the subject of controversy.

Sometimes, national history takes the form of propaganda, in which leaders or elites use biased or misleading information to control or influence their citizens or followers in a particular way. In this way, history is used as a tool. Propaganda is

---

[30] Benedict Anderson, *Imagined communities—Reflections on the Origin and Spread of Nationalism*, Verso, 1983, rev. ed. 2006.

widely used during times of high stress for a nation (e.g., war), but it is also used at other times.

Probably one of the best examples of the strong link between propaganda and history comes from the Soviet Union under the leadership of Josef Stalin. These four pictures show the same scene, but with different people in it! This means that the history was changed over time. In the first photograph (top left), Stalin is standing with three other colleagues or comrades (Antipov, Kirov, Shvernik). However, in the second picture (top right), one of the comrades has been removed. In the third picture (bottom left), another has been removed. By the

Figure 3 Manipulated photo of Stalin.

final picture (bottom right), only Stalin remains. The other three people have been erased from this record of history. In this way, Stalin has tried to change history, by putting only himself at the centre of history, and thus trying to strengthen his rule. It is easy for governments that can control the mass media to use propaganda. It is more difficult for governments of countries that have an independent mass media.

At other times, it is possible to see how the individual preferences or biases of leaders makes them propose differing views of history. Which views become dominant can be very important in terms of social and political outcomes. Consider the following two passages. They are both recent statements about Japan's experiences in the Second World War, and what happened after the war, but they choose very different interpretations of the events. Further, it seems entirely possible that the interpretations that each suggest lead to very different ideas about what should happen in the present and future.

Activity: Ideological statements and history

- Abe Shinzo, the Prime Minister of Japan, said the following in a speech commemorating the end of the war on the 14th of August 2015:

"The peace we enjoy today exists only upon such precious sacrifices [3 million Japanese war dead]. And therein lies the origin of post-war Japan."

- The following day, on the 15th of August 2015, in another speech commemorating the end of the war, the Japanese monarch, Akihito, said the following:

"Our country today enjoys peace and prosperity, thanks to the ceaseless efforts made by the people of Japan toward recovery from the devastation of the war and toward development, always backed by their earnest desire for the continuation of peace."

- *These two statements show a very different understanding of history, with very different implications for the future. Can you explain how / why?*

Abe Shinzo would like to make Japan a regular country, with a regular military that can be used overseas. For him, what is important is the spirit of sacrifice shown, for example, by the soldiers who sacrificed their lives for the monarch Hirohito. That spirit, he suggests, is what post-war Japan is based on. The implication, then, is that it would be good for Japanese to re-discover that same spirit of self-sacrifice and public spirit today, in an age when narrow-minded profit-seeking and private aims have become very important, even as ageing and economic decline weaken Japan's power. Thus, if his version of history were to become mainstream, we might expect to see the strengthening of nationalistic education, and the encouragement of nationalistic acts, in an attempt to maintain Japan's status as a major regional power now and into the future.

Akihito's speech presents a rather different interpretation of history. In his case, Japan's present is based on a rejection of war-time Japan, and a strong commitment to hard work and peace. His perspective on history suggests that it is important not to change these key points and implies that it would not be good to reinforce nationalism that promotes self-sacrifice for country, or to turn the Self-Defence Forces into a regular military force. If Akihito's version of history becomes dominant, then ageing and shrinking Japan may be more likely to become something like a Switzerland of the East.

While you may think neither statement is precisely "propaganda", it is at the least obvious that neither one is precisely "correct" or "the truth". Rather, historical facts—war, defeat, reconstruction, peace and prosperity—are put into different stories, with different intentions and messages in mind. Because different political forces try to use history to achieve their own ends, in order for us to make free and rational decisions and judgments, it is very important that we have sufficient historical knowledge of our own. Only by being well-informed can we critically consider what different parties and governments claim.

Often, state history education is insufficient for this purpose, as governments may try to promote certain kinds of history over others. Nationalist governments often try to whitewash or conceal certain events, while emphasizing others. Politicians in general will try to do the same: they will emphasize their successes and strong points but will prefer not to deal with their failures and weak points in detail, if at all. Academic history provides us with assistance in perceiving and countering such biases.

Overcoming national history

For reasons relating to nation-formation and also political rivalry, it sometimes happens that neighbouring countries develop very different understandings of shared historical events. A good example can be found in North-East Asia, where Japan, China, Taiwan, and the two Koreas may agree on many facts of what happened in the region from the late-19th century into the Cold War era but have quite different understandings of the significance and meaning of those facts. To engage in an in-depth discussion of war-time history is beyond the scope of this chapter, but the following general points have been pointed out with regard to history teaching about the war in these countries.[31]

- *Japanese textbooks tend to give a simple chronological account and avoid talking about why war broke out and whose responsibility it was. It presents the Japanese people as victims of military and government deception.*
  This version allows the Japanese nation to believe in itself as "good", while allowing for silence on the question of war responsibility.
- *Korean textbooks frame the war as leading towards Korean political independence and nation-state formation. Why and how the war ended, Korean-Japanese cooperation ("collaboration"), and the so-called "positive" economic effects of Japan's colonization are not treated in any detail.*
  The unity of the Korean nation is established in opposition to Japan. Partly as a result, the complicated relationships that existed between colonizer and colonized in the Japanese empire are ignored.
- *In Taiwan, after criticism of the "glorification" of Japanese colonialism and anti-Chinese bias, history textbooks now mention Japanese colonial rule's economic benefits, as well as colonial-era discrimination against Taiwanese people. On the other hand, comfort women are not covered.*
  Taiwanese nation-building involved establishing a Taiwanese identity both against Japan and against China.
- *Chinese history textbooks formerly stressed how evil Japan was, focusing on events like the Nanking massacre. Recently, however, the quantity of such descriptions has been reduced, and Japan's success in post-Meiji modernization, as well as development aid to countries including China, is commonly praised.*

31 Gotelind Muller, *Designing history in East Asian Textbooks*, Routledge, 2011; Isabel Barca and Irene Nakou, *Contemporary public debates over history education*, IAP, 2010; Karina V. Korostelina and Simone Lässig eds., *History education and post-conflict reconciliation*, Routledge, 2013; Kevin P. Clements, ed., *Identity, trust, and reconciliation in East Asia*, Palgrave Macmillan 2018.

China's unity and goodness was partly defined by stressing its opposition with "evil" Japan. China's rise to global political and economic power, and Japan's relative decline, may be changing this strategy.

In the early 2000s, Japanese, South Korean and Chinese members of a non-governmental academic society began a project to develop a common history textbook of the East Asian region, entitled A History that Opens the Future.[32] In so doing, it became necessary to write about the Japanese people as both victimizers and victims, in a way that was acceptable to Chinese, Korean, and Japanese participants in the project. More controversial was the role of the United States in the post-WWII region: for Korea and Japan, it tends to be seen as the source of liberal democracy and human rights and freedom; for China, it is more often seen as an aggressive threat to world peace; for dissenters within Japan and Korea, the US supported military dictatorship in Korea and made Japan a collaborator in the Korean and Vietnam wars. Overall, observers think that this kind of textbook reveals the narrowmindedness that exists in all national histories, but also that peaceful and respectful dialogue about different views is both possible and desirable, and that there is not necessarily only one "correct" version of history.

History can be a symphony of different voices in dialogue, rather than in harmony. Of course, in countries with freedom of speech, it may be more possible to make the "truth" clear, since different points of view are more likely to be exchanged in public, with an open debate over who has the best-supported point of view. At the same time, freedom of speech generally involves diversity of opinion, and so we can probably never achieve consensus on the meaning of history.

An interesting background issue here is the fact that Korea, Taiwan, China, and Japan are becoming ever more closely integrated economically, and even culturally too. Despite this, however, the fact that they are divided into nation-states, which have a national focus, means that politically and socially, there is a tendency to stress the differences between them. In the future, however, if political integration ever progresses, then we may see the creation of an East Asian history in which events will be included for their significance in terms of realizing an integrated East Asian region, rather than in terms of their importance for a particular nation-state.

---

[32] In Japanese, 日中韓 3 国共通歴史教材委員会,『未来をひらく歴史—東アジア三国の近現代史』, 高文研, 2006.

History and human nature

When we study history, we learn what humans have done over many years, in many different places. Importantly, we don't just learn about general principles, but also about individual people and events. We learn about people who do great things and people who do awful things, people who face hardship with incredible dignity, and people who find hope even in the most unlikely of situations. This list of significant figures in history should make this point obvious.

Table 9 Famous historical figures
1 Jesus
2 Napoleon
3 Muhammad
William Shakespeare
5 Abraham Lincoln
6 George Washington
7 Adolf Hitler
8 Aristotle
9 Alexander the Great
10 Thomas Jefferson
38 Genghis Khan
6 Mohandas Karamchand Gandhi
52 Gautama Buddha.

Steven Skiena and Charles B. Ward, *Who's Bigger? Where Historical Figures Really Rank*, Cambridge

Activity: Human diversity

- *Kant thought that the diversity of human existence revealed that we are quite deeply flawed, affected by vanity, wickedness, egotism, ignorance. What do you think? Was he right? Is this all there is to say about human diversity? What might we add based on this list of historical figures?*
- *The playwright Terence of Rome was a freed slave who lived in the second century B.C. One of his most famous statements is, in the original Latin, "Homo sum, humani nihil a me alienum puto," or in English, "I am a man, I consider nothing that is human alien to me." How might the study of history help us to grasp this idea, and why is it an important idea to hold?*

Activity: Towards a more peaceful world?

- *Watch the TED talk by Steven Pinker called, "The surprising decline in violence". What lifestyles or values have changed over time?*

Explaining the present

It is obvious that the world of today has been made by the past. "Today's news" is built from "Yesterday's news". This means that if we want to have any real understanding of the world in which we live, we must study history. Let's look at some examples.

In Japan today, Article 9 of the Constitution seems to be very highly valued by a considerable proportion of the population. Many (perhaps half according to some surveys) Japanese people don't want this to be changed. Article 9 prohibits

Japan from having any military. It says, "...land, sea, and air forces, as well as other war potential, will never be maintained." This seems to be very clear. According to the Constitution, Japan must have no military. Yet, Japan has one of the most advanced militaries in the world. This means that the Self-Defence Force (SDF) is unconstitutional or illegal, at least if it is defined as "war potential". To define the SDF as not having the potential to be used in war may seem unreasonable given its size and capabilities (although this argument has been made by the Japanese government). A more interesting argument would be that the Japanese government *has no intention* of using the SDF in war, and so the SDF forces *are not war potential*. However, any and all countries could say the same thing. Anyway, while supporting Article 9, it seems that most people in Japan also respect and support the SDF. How do we explain this strange phenomenon? Well, we cannot explain it unless we look at history, and especially the history of WWII.

Especially, we need to look at things such as: a) the US authorities' inclusion of Article 9 in the Constitution after World War II to make sure they never had to fight another war with Japan (actually, some consider that Article 9 originated with the Japanese government of the time); b) the rapid realization by the U.S. that this had been a bad idea, given the development of the Cold War and the potential value of Japanese troops as allies in the U.S. Cold War strategy; c) growing U.S. support for the re-militarization of Japan, and consequently, U.S. support for the LDP, which supported remilitarization; d) the post-war Japanese population's clear preference for pacifism. Together, these factors meant that partial re-militarization turned out to be possible, but constitutional change did not, giving rise to the contradictory situation that exists today.

The current government proposes to resolve this contradiction by changing the Constitution to regularize the SDF and recognize it as a normal military force. Constitutional fundamentalists propose to resolve the problem by eliminating the SDF. Most fall somewhere in between those two poles.

To take another example, Okinawa covers less than 1% of the land surface of Japan yet hosts over 60% of the US military in Japan. Not surprisingly, most Okinawans do not like this situation. 85 percent of Okinawans are opposed to the presence of the U.S. military, according to a 2007 survey. A 2010 survey by the Asahi Shimbun found that 43 percent of the Okinawan population wanted the complete closure of all U.S. bases, 42 percent wanted a reduction in the US military, and only 11 percent wanted no change. So, the people of Okinawa carry an unfair burden of the US military in Japan, and they want this changed. Many Japanese people agree that the situation is unfair, and the Hatoyama government (2009-2010) promised to improve the situation but collapsed before achieving meaningful change.

How do we explain Okinawa's situation? Well, we must understand the history of Okinawa's integration by force into Japan in 1879, the assimilation policy that was introduced, and mainland Japanese discrimination against Okinawans. We must understand the history of US-Japan relations, especially the post-WWII era, when the U.S. maintained its control over Okinawa until 1972, 20 years after the main Japanese islands regained sovereignty. We would need to know about the Okinawan decision to seek re-incorporation into Japan in order to achieve independence from U.S. rule and to obtain the protections and freedoms guaranteed by the post-war Japanese Constitution. Further, we would also need to be aware of the effects of Japanese subordination to U.S. hegemony in the Cold War and post-Cold War, with Japan giving the U.S. freedom to use its Okinawan bases immediately after Okinawan reversion in return for U.S. security guarantees.

There are many complex issues in the world around us. Finding solutions to them requires understanding, which requires historical knowledge about how the problems were created.

Activity: Poster presentation project

- *Identity a current issue in Japan's international relations. Research the development of this issue, creating a timeline showing significant events and actors, and indicating the relationships between them.*

Part 2. Methodology: How to study the past

So, having looked at what history is and why we should study it, we must now look at *how* we study history. Obviously, the past is the past and so it is gone, forever. Objectively, we cannot change it. So, how do we learn about what happened, and more importantly, perhaps, why something happened, many years ago? How do we look into the past?

Historians are like detectives who want to find out the truth about a crime: we must find out the who and the what, as well as the how and why and when. We must look for reliable *evidence* that we can trust. When we do this, we must be *objective*, and try to be aware of our prejudices and biases. We must use our objective, rational brain, when we look at the evidence. Evidence from history, or historical evidence, can be divided into two main types, primary sources and secondary sources.

Primary Sources

Basically, primary sources are evidence given by someone who was present *at the time* of the event. Any diary you wrote when you were a high school student is a primary source of your time as a high school student, and of high school life in the 2000s. In the same way, your grandmother's diary when she was a high school student is also a primary source of her time as a high school student, and of high school life during the era when she was a student. The "Kokin Wakashu" is a collection of poems from the Heian period. They were written between 905 and about 920AD, by four court poets. The Kokin Wakashu poems are primary sources of court life in that time.

We can see therefore, that primary sources are 'first-hand', made at the time by someone who was there. Primary sources are necessary to study and understand the past. History cannot be studied without using primary sources. Indeed, secondary sources must use primary sources. For example, there is a book called "Genbaku Taikenki", which was edited by Oe Kenzaburo. It was first published in 1965, so it is not a primary source. However, the book is full of stories told by people who were in Hiroshima when the atom bombs were dropped in August 1945. So, the book is full of primary sources.

Primary source problems: Individual filters

We have said that primary sources are necessary evidence for us in our study of history. However, we must be careful with primary sources. There are a number of reasons why primary sources may not be 100% reliable. The first one relates to the individuality of eyewitnesses.

People make mistakes. People see things differently. People have biases and prejudices. People have different interests and different backgrounds. Imagine that we read several diaries about the same historical event. It is very likely that we would have very different stories of that one same event.

When someone writes a diary, they must decide what to write and what not to write: the filter of each eyewitness decides what will be included, and what will be excluded. They must decide how to write about something, or in other words, which words to use, and which words to avoid. All of this will be different for different people.

Of course, we should say that if you read several diaries of the same historical event, it is very likely that you would get a *general picture* of what happened. You might not understand *why* things happened (which is the most important purpose of historical study), but you would have some understanding of the reality of the historical event.

Social Bias

Another issue with primary sources is that they are likely to tell us more about some types of people and information than others. Consider the case of early-modern history, for example. Illiterate farmers don't leave any trace of their existence in writing, so we won't find texts by them. We do find lots of texts written by government officials and religious officials. However, government officials were interested in things like population, agricultural productivity, and taxation, while religious officials were interested in religious matters such as the number of believers, how much income they received, and so on. So, using primary sources that they produced gives us information on some topics, but not about everything. Using such sources, we need to remember that they only tell a part of the story, from a limited perspective. For other kinds of information, we might look to, for example, poems, novels, and theatre of the time. Archaeological research, for example into rubbish dumps or people's remains, also has the potential to tell us a lot about the lifestyles of ordinary premodern people.

Shared beliefs are another form of social bias that affect the reliability of historical sources. All social groups have some social biases, which members believe to varying degrees. Importantly, these social biases often become part of national identity, and so there is a link between social bias and nationalism. Racism is a very good example of this. Generally speaking, racism is the belief that one race is superior to another race. It is a kind of prejudiced belief. We should first say that "race" is an old idea, but it has no scientific basis. "Races" do not exist in any natural or scientific way since internal genetic diversity in each "race" is much greater than the diversity between "races". Rather, "race" is a socially constructed idea, based on choosing certain aspects of the way people look—mainly hair and skin—as being particularly significant. Even Carl Linnaeus, the 18th century creator of our system for scientifically classifying living things, was a believer in the idea that there existed human races.

Until at least the second half of the 20th century, many people, including great intellectuals, politicians and scientists, believed that white people were superior to non-whites. Gandhi is considered to have believed that black Africans were inferior to Indians, while more recently, James Watson, who won a Nobel Prize for his work on DNA, is notorious for his racist views that white people are smarter than black people. Such racist beliefs have had a variety of consequences in the real world.

Firstly, as the social bias of racism developed and spread, it became a justification for colonialism and imperial domination. Europeans, and later Japanese and Americans, thought that they were superior to the people they colonized, and that this superiority gave them the right and sometimes even the responsibility to colonize and govern others. Indeed, members of the Kyoto School, a group of philosophers based at Kyoto University, were criticized for supporting the ideas of racial superiority that were held by the military during the period of Japanese colonialism. It was a social bias of that time.

Describe this cartoon: what are the different countries represented here? What kinds of bias concerning them can you see?

Figure 4 1898 French Cartoon.

How does this relate to doing history? In reading what Japanese eyewitnesses of the colonial era and afterwards wrote about Korea and Koreans, it would be necessary to take into account the existence of widespread prejudices against Korea. Similarly, in reading war-time American texts about Japan, it is necessary to keep in mind that American thinking was strongly affected by anti-Japanese racism.

In the case of some sources, such as wartime propaganda, it becomes necessary to keep in mind that the material is affected not only by unconscious bias, but also deliberate bias. For example, a lot of war propaganda deliberately tries to dehumanize the enemy by showing them to be animals or subhuman, and so raises motivation to fight them, and also makes it easier to kill the "enemy".[33]

---

[33] John Dower's *War without mercy,* Pantheon, 1987, looks at many examples of wartime propaganda used by the U.S. and Japan during the Pacific War.

So, while primary sources are essential to any study of history, we must carefully consider the weaknesses of such evidence. In particular, the filters and biases of witnesses are an important issue that must be kept in mind.

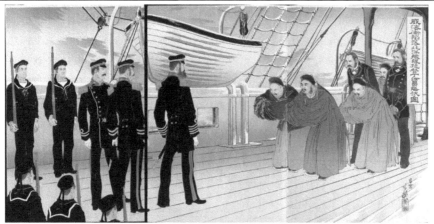

Figure 5 Migita Toshihide, *Surrender of Chinese Forces after the Battle of Weihaiwei,* 1895.

What messages does this picture suggest about 1. The Japanese, 2. The Chinese, and 3. Westerners? What kinds of bias is revealed?

Activity: The reliability of sources

- *In thinking about the reliability of a source, we need to consider issues such as:*
A) *The writer or producer (who made it)*
B) *The date it was made (when)*
C) *The place that it comes from (where)*
D) *The reason why the source was made (why)*
E) *The intended audience of the source? (who / why)*

Example: the 1989 Tiananmen Square Massacre (June 4th Incident)	What limitations might the following sources have?
Source A: an extract from the autobiography of an eyewitness to the 1989 Tiananmen Square incident, published in Beijing in 2010. The witness was born in 1930.	
Source B: an extract from the People's Daily, a Chinese government newspaper, dated 6 June 1989.	
Source C: an extract from John Smith, *China in the Twentieth Century*, 2001. John Smith is a well-known writer of school history textbooks.	
Source D: an extract from the diary of a Chinese woman killed on 4 June in Tiananmen Square as she was taking part in a protest demonstration, published in New York in 2008.	

Secondary Sources

When a historian writes a history of something, this is a secondary source of historical evidence. Most of what we read about history is this type of secondary source. Of course, historians must use primary sources, but their purpose is to *explain* and *interpret* the event. The historian aims to show *what* happens and analyse that event to also explain *why* it happened; to explain its *meaning*.

How does a historian choose what to write about? Well, firstly that depends on the interests of the historian: they choose sources depending on what they want to explain, or what argument they want to make. In making this decision, they are influenced by a combination of individual interests and ideologies, as well as by the social context in which they exist. But, it also depends on the historical sources available—it's quite difficult to write about things for which there is no evidence. This means that the writers of secondary sources select what they write from the evidence provided by writers of primary sources, who themselves selected what they would write. Consequently, a double selection lies behind the creation of secondary sources. This means that history is not all that happened in the past, but only a selection of what happened in the past. You already subconsciously know this: there is no way that a book of a few hundred pages can cover the whole of a single person's life, let alone a war or an era of one or several countries!

Indeed, given that historians engage in the manipulation of a very complex past into a relatively simple narrative, we should say here that perhaps historians *create* history when they write history. There is a relatively popular argument today that the writing of historical narrative is not all that different from the writing of fictional narrative.[34]

Hindsight

One of the unusual characteristics of history is that people write after the event. Therefore, they write knowing what has happened. They write, in other words, with the benefit of *hindsight*. Often, decisions about what to include in or exclude from history are based on this: knowing that X happened, all the things that appear to lead to X become significant. But this may be a problem for actually understanding the actions and thinking of people at the time, since they didn't have the benefit of hindsight, and could not know that what they did would lead to X.

---

[34] See, for example, Ann Curthoys and John Docker, eds., *Is history fiction?* University of Michigan, rev.ed. 2015.

In our own lives, we often use hindsight when we look back and judge decisions we have made in the past. When we do this, we may give those decisions a significance that they did not have at the time. To take an everyday example, say one of your school classmates becomes a famous politician in the future. Knowing this, you may recall about that classmate's school days that she or he "always loved to debate", or "liked nothing more than to be in charge of things". Characteristics of that former classmate that seem connected to that person becoming a politician in the present are retrieved from your memory and presented as significant historical evidence of the political destiny of your classmate. And while this evidence may be "true", it is evidence that appears significant because of hindsight.

The labelling of eras or periods is also something that is done with the benefit of hindsight. To people who lived in the late-15th and 16th centuries, it may not have been obvious that they lived in the Age of Exploration. Similarly, to people in the 19th and early 20th century, it may not have been obvious that they lived in the Age of Imperialism. It is only to us today, looking back, that these labels seem obvious.

While hindsight helps us to place past events into a narrative, it can also cause a kind of bias. For example, during the Cold War, no-one would have predicted the rise of terrorism to the status of a global issue. When we look back now at the end of the Cold War, it seems to have been inevitable that Communism would fail. But, at the time, almost no-one predicted the end of the Cold War or the collapse of the Soviet Union.[35]

Similarly, the decision taken by the Japanese government in 1941 to attack the U.S. Navy in Pearl Harbor now looks like a reckless choice that ended in disaster for Japan. A simple comparison of the levels of production just of the US and Japan for military equipment, as well as related resources, during World War II makes this look obvious to us now. But to think that disaster was just as predictable for leaders in 1941 as for us today is to fall into the trap of *hindsight bias*.

Table 10 Japanese and U.S. wartime power

WWII production levels	Japan	USA (all fronts)
Aircraft (all types)	76,000	300,000
Aircraft carriers (all types)	16	163
All other warships	241	1,028
Trucks	165,000	2,400,000
Tanks	2,500	88,500

---

[35] The famous exception was the French demographer Emmanuel Todd, who predicted the downfall of the U.S.S.R. based on population statistics in his book *La chute finale*, or *The final fall*, Robert Laffont, 1976.

Atomic bombs	0	3
Coal (tonnes)	185,000,000	2,100,000,000
Iron ore (tonnes)	21,000,000	400,000,000
Petroleum (tonnes)	5,000,000	830,000,000

Hindsight also tells us that as a result of this war, around 3 million Japanese died, Japan lost almost all its overseas colonies, and about one quarter of its machines, equipment, buildings, and houses were destroyed. Ironically, ultra-nationalism and anti-communism had been two driving forces for the war, but the war eventually led to a social-democratic revolution in Japan, the rise of communism in China, and Japan's occupation by the Allied military forces.[36]

If we cancel out the knowledge we get from hindsight, though, the war against the U.S. may look rather different. Let's have a look at some of the statements by people involved in the decision to attack Pearl Harbor, to clarify this point.

Activity: Doing history—the decision to go to war with the U.S. in 1941[37]

Tōjō Hideki (Prime Minister)

On the basis of the Imperial Conference decision of November 5, the Army and Navy devoted themselves to getting everything ready for war, while the Government used every means and made every effort to improve diplomatic relations with the United States. The United States refused to make any concessions and demanded complete withdrawal of troops from China. This violated the dignity of our Empire and made it impossible for us to enjoy the fruits of the China Incident, and also threatened the very existence of our Empire. It became evident that we could not achieve our goals by means of diplomacy.

● For Tōjō, what is the problem with the U.S. demands? Explain with reference to Japanese actions on the continent during the 1930s.

At the same time, the United States, Great Britain, the Netherlands, and China increased their economic and military pressure against us; and we have now reached the point where we can no longer allow the situation to continue, from the point of view of both our national power and our planned military operations. Moreover, the requirements with respect to military operations will not permit an extension of time. Under the

---

[36] Kenneth Pyle, *The making of modern Japan*, Wadsworth, 1996.
[37] Statements from an Imperial conference with Hirohito in attendance, held on the 1st December 1941. Wm. Theodore de Bary, *Sources of Japanese Tradition: Volume 2, 1600 to 2000*, Columbia University Press, 2005. (Sources edited for simplicity).

circumstances, our Empire has no alternative but to begin war against the
United States, Great Britain, and the Netherlands in order to resolve the
present crisis and assure survival....

- Tōjō also talks about how "our national power and our projected military operations" mean that war is the only option. What does he mean? (Think about what a lengthy economic blockade would mean for Japan's military and state power).

Tōgō Shigenori (Minister for Foreign and Colonial Affairs)

The United States Government has stuck to its traditional positions,
ignored realities in East Asia, and tried to force our Empire to agree to
unacceptable demands. Despite the fact that we made a number of
concessions, the U.S. maintained its position throughout the negotiations
and refused any change at all. America's policy toward Japan has
consistently been to stop the establishment of a New Order in East Asia,
which is our unchangeable policy. We must recognize that if we were to
accept their present proposal, the international position of our Empire
would be reduced to a status lower than it was prior to the Manchurian
incident, and our very survival would inevitably be threatened....

To what extent is Tōgō's reasoning different to, and similar to, Tōjō's?

Hara Yoshimichi (Privy Council President)

We are reluctant to make our people to suffer even greater hardships, on
top of what they have endured during the four years since the China
incident. But it is clear that the existence of our country is being
threatened, that the great achievements of the Emperor Meiji would all
come to nothing, and that there is nothing else we can do. I believe that the
proposal before us [for war] cannot be avoided in the light of present
circumstances, and I put my trust in officers and men whose loyalty is
supreme. I urge you to make every effort to keep the people in a tranquil
state of mind, in order to carry on a long-term war.

- What does Hara worry about? How should we understand his reference to "the people" needing to be kept "in a tranquil state of mind"?

In some ways hindsight helps us to be wise after the event, but does that really help us to understand why the event happened in the first place? Does hindsight help us to understand the decision made at the time? Is hindsight just another bias we need to be careful of?

We should add one more point regarding the problem of hindsight. Hindsight itself is constantly changing, as our knowledge and interests evolve. What used to be generally believed may change, or even be overturned, and so events will be reviewed as a result. History becomes a kind of constantly revised dialogue between the period that it deals with, and the period in which it is written.

Activity: Using hindsight

- *Use hindsight to think again about an important decision you took in your own personal history.*
- *What do you think our current age will be called, in 200 years' time? If your era label becomes widely used, what kinds of things will appear significant? What kinds of things will lose significance?*

Part 3 Bias and history

When we either write or read history, it is important that we consider the impact of biases. We have talked a little about biases in the section on sources, but we will now focus on general biases that affect the study of history.

Topic choice bias

How do historians choose what history they write about? The interests of the present affect what history we study or write about. After the 2008-2009 financial crisis, historians showed renewed interest in the 1929 financial crisis. The recent rise of populist political forces around the world has encouraged historians to reconsider the rise of fascism and national socialism in the 1920s and 1930s. Environmental disaster in China today is encouraging greater interest in the contemporary history of Japan, which also experienced massive environmental pollution during its period of rapid economic growth. The growing influence of the belief that democracy is in trouble today has led many scholars to look back at the history of democratic thinking and practice, and especially at Athenian democracy in classical Greece. The fact that historians tend to choose topics which reflect the interests and issues of their society and era is a kind of topic choice bias. However, whether the history that is then written is affected by further biases is separate issue.

Confirmation Bias

Humans have a tendency to see only that which confirms the things they already believe in. This means that often, people selectively focus on information according to what they already believe in. This tendency, known as "confirmation bias" is especially strong when emotions are also strong. Because humans do this, then historians could also do it when they study history. They could have a preferred theory about a historical event, and when they investigate that event, they might notice only evidence that supports their view, and ignore evidence that does not.

Thus, historians who take the view that the French Revolution led to the spread of democracy and freedom around the world may prefer to overlook evidence about sexism and racism and xenophobia shown by the people who made the Revolution happen. Similarly, historians who are interested in the Meiji Restoration as an event that led to the return of monarchical rule in Japan may choose to downplay the way in which many of the institutions and traditions of the contemporary Japanese monarchy are modern, having been invented during the Meiji era.[38] In order to avoid these kinds of issues, a good historian, like any good scientist, must actively look for evidence that goes against their beliefs.

National Bias

Nation-states encourage their populations to have nationalist beliefs and to value the national communities that they belong to. Because a nation is an emotional community more than a rational community, people tend to have problems thinking about their own and other nations objectively. To get an idea of the problem, you might like to watch or listen to a television broadcast of an important World Cup football game involving Japan. If you listen to the Japanese commentators, you will surely notice that they have great trouble being calm and objective. In fact, they tend to be more like a group of biased supporters than rational commentators. This kind of emotional national identification can also affect historians.

Nationalistic emotions can make historians seek things they can be proud of and ignore things that they think are shameful. U.S. historians may try to justify the atomic bombings, or the Iraq War, or the Afghan War, while Japanese historians may try to justify colonizing Korea, invading China, incorporating Ezo (Hokkaido) and Ryukyu (Okinawa) into modern Japan, making an organized system to provide soldiers with women for sex during the Second World War, and so on. Further,

---

[38] Takashi Fujitani, *Splendid monarchy: power and pageantry in modern Japan*, University of California Press, 1998.

because of these kinds of nationalist biases, U.S. historians who describe how the Hiroshima and Nagasaki atomic bombings were unnecessary, or Japanese historians who describe the evils of the military system to provide soldiers with women for sex, may find that they are labelled "traitors". However, as historians engage in dialogue across national borders more and more, and as societies and histories become more transnational, major national biases may be overcome.

Activity: National biases

- *Is the existence of a national bias one reason why it is so difficult to change Japan's constitution?*
- *Is it rational, to feel shame or pride in what some people did long ago, just because you share a passport / nationality / country of residence with them? Is it rational to feel shame or pride in what some people do today, just because you share a passport / nationality / country of residence with them?*

Overcoming bias with multi-factor histories

Finally, it is important to consider that historical events are complex, and therefore describing or explaining their cause or causes is rarely simple. Working out how many causes were involved, and how they were involved, as well as how each cause was related to other causes, is a highly complicated operation.

Activity: Causes of historical events

- *Suggest at least six major causes of Japan's defeat by China, the United States, and other allied forces in World War II. Was any more important than the others?*

Although we like to look for decisive causes, or the most important causes, it is often not possible to identify just one or two things that made all the difference. Rather, we may try to separate historical factors into various levels or categories, so we can try to explain an event systematically from multiple perspectives.

Activity: Categorizing causes of historical events

- *Classify the causes of Japan's defeat by China, the U.S. and other allied forces in World War II into the following categories, adding any new factors that you think of.*

Geography	Society	Economy	Individual motivations	Chance

Many historians are relatively confident that the organized or systematic narratives that they produce about the past—history—describe how and explain why something happened pretty accurately. They also believe that the study of history can help us to generalize about human societies through time. However, both of these positions face some serious criticisms.

Are the narratives that historians write "reliable" and "unbiased? Historians actually cannot avoid making biased narratives, because using the same historical evidence, you can write more than one coherent story. So long as people hold different beliefs about society, economy, and politics, it is unavoidable that they will create different historical narratives. A common example used to illustrate this point is the contrast between the so-called Whig or liberal view and the Tory or conservative view of British history. Whig history focused on the development of freedoms and democracy in Britain. Their history was linear and focused on progress as a law of history. In contrast, the Tory view of history focussed on the importance of accident and chance. This was because unintended consequences were common, and people often are unable to achieve their aims.[39] Using the same material, Whigs and Tories created two contrasting histories—one of an organized history that moves towards progress, and another of a history of more random events. Neither can be said to be "wrong" or "right". Rather, they are the result of using different frameworks for understanding history.

Whether generalizations from history are justified is also controversial. Every event—a life, a war, a crisis—happens in a unique environment made by a unique set of factors. A single change in any of the factors may have resulted in a different outcome. Does studying the American Revolution lead to insights into the French revolution and the Arab Spring? Does studying Japan's Pacific War tell us much about the Vietnam War, or about wars in general? Can the history of Japan's economic development help us to understand economic development in Korea, Taiwan, or Vietnam? Given how complex every event is, it would be equally possible to (a) find a wide range of differences by looking for what made each event special, and (b) find a wide range of similarities by looking for what various events have in common. Obviously, in considering economic development, war, or revolution, the more we zoom in, the more likely it is that we will notice differences, and the more we zoom out, the more likely it is that we will notice similarities. Scholars who want to deeply understand a single event will prefer the first approach, while scholars who are more interested in laws and theories about history will prefer the second approach.

---

[39] Kagan, *op. cit.*

Part 4 Theories of History

As we have already said, the purpose of studying history is to explain the past. When we study the past, we usually do not begin each time without any assumptions about the past, or about how we should study it. Usually, we have some ideas about what happened and why—we may have a loose outline or even a theory about what happened. A theory is basically an explanation of how something works. A theory of history is a kind of explanation about why and how things happened in the past.

Geographical determinism

Among the theories that are relevant to the study of history is that of *geo-history*, a framework associated with the French historian Fernand Braudel.[40] He developed this idea in his studies of the Mediterranean region, looking at how areas with similar climates, linked by the sea in secure times, and isolated by the sea in insecure times, developed partly as a result of their environment, and partly as a result of human modification of the environment.

Another example comes from the British Isles. At the beginning of the Industrial Revolution, Britain had plenty of coal to use as energy for the new industries. Britain also had fertile soil so agriculture was productive. Furthermore, as an island nation, trade by sea was relatively inexpensive. Connected to this is the large number of navigable rivers that made domestic trade relatively cheap. All these are geographical factors that helped Britain to industrialize. In short, Britain's central role in the industrial age is explained as a factor of its natural geography.

Activity: Geography in Asian history

- *What effect has geography had on the history of Japan? What about Korea? China? The U.S.?*

Cyclical Theories

A cycle goes around and around, so according to cyclical theories of history, history goes around and around, repeating itself. One common pattern is that of the rise and fall of civilizations, or great powers. When one civilization falls, another replaces it. One state rises to become powerful, then falls, and is replaced by another

---

[40] See, for example, Fernand Braudel, *The Mediterranean and the Mediterranean world in the age of Philip II, vol. 1,* University of California Press, 1995. Jared Diamond is another well-known scholar who looks at how geographical factors determine the course of history in different contexts. See his *Guns, germs, and steel,* W.W. Norton, 1997.

state. According to this idea, there is no real progress, only a repeating pattern. Understanding the pattern enables understanding of history.

These kinds of frameworks are used to think about the rise and fall of the Roman empire, the British empire, and the recent American empire too. Graeme Allison has drawn notice recently for his views on the U.S. as a falling power, and China as a rising power. Allison uses history to argue that when a major power is falling and another major power is rising, there is a high risk of a war occurring between the two, and that the U.S.-China relationship is therefore a very risky one.[41]

Linear Theories

Linear means "in a straight line", so the linear theory of history argues that history *progresses* in a single direction, towards "enlightenment". History is about the progress of humans, perhaps beginning when apes came down from the trees and became early humans. History is then the story of human development, not just economic development, but social and political development too. Each age improves on the previous one, with the current age characterized, according to Steven Pinker, by a massive reduction in the level of violence, and ever greater respect for human rights. Pinker notes, for example, the following progression.[42] (His narrative may remind you of the Whig view of history.)

Table 11 The decline in violent death through history

	Pre-state societies	Middle ages	Worldwide today	Europe today
Violent deaths per 100,000 people *per year*	500	50	6	1

Great Person Theories

According to this theory, history is shaped by great leaders. Leaders make the important decisions that affect history. In this way, leaders determine what happens. Certainly, leaders want to determine what happens. But can we agree that leaders make all the difference? Probably not.

Today, the great person theory is mainly popular with readers of historical romances who apparently enjoy the stories of "heroes" of the past who shape history.

---

[41] Graeme T. Allison, *Destined for war: can America and China escape Thucydides' trap?*, Scribe, 2017.
[42] Steven Pinker, *The better angels of our nature*, Viking, 2011; *Enlightenment now—the case for reason, science, humanism, and progress*, Viking, 2018. .

Great person theory personalizes history by making a single person or several people the major actors of history, instead of complex social, economic, and political processes, so that history feels easier to understand. But few serious historians think that individuals determine the course of history. Of course, it is important to understand what leaders thought and believed, in order to understand their decisions and actions. But such individuals can only be understood as pieces of a larger system, with the international and state environments determining much of what they do.

No matter how great a military leader is, without technological and human resources, they cannot win battles. No matter how brilliant a politician is, without state power, they cannot affect the course of world history. Without the insights of the people before them, and the support of people around them, no genius would ever get the chance to demonstrate their genius. Further, no individual can avoid the influence of their social environment.

Activity: Great people in history

● *Is history decided by great figures such as Napoleon, Bismarck, Lenin, De Gaulle and Churchill? Or do great figures become great only because the wider socio-economic context allows them to?*

Economic Determinism

Karl Marx said that history is driven by technological innovation and economic systems. These determine social organization, and social organization determines how people think. For example, innovation in tools and seed technology allowed the rise of agricultural societies, which caused specific changes in social organization and thinking compared to previous hunter-gatherer and pastoral societies. Industrial societies too, are based on new technologies, and their societies are differently organized, and what people think is also different to past socio-economic systems. Today's information society, based on rapid communications technology and increasingly on machine learning, is probably going to result in societies that are no longer organized around mass work and salaried work. Thus, people's values and social norms are also likely to change in a revolutionary way!

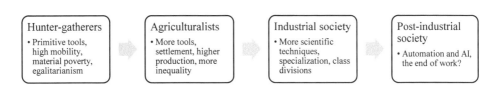

Figure 6 Technological change and social change

- *How was society organized in Japan's Edo period? What kind of economic system did it have? What were the technological foundations of Edo society? How did people think about time, work, and money? How did Japan's society and economy change in the Meiji period? Why?*
- *Are technological innovations such as the printing press, the steam engine, and the computer more important than any individual great people?*

Conclusion

In this chapter we have looked at studying history. First of all, we asked the question, what is history? The answer is that history is not just the past, but a selection of the past. What part of the past is history? Well, when we look at history we usually look at significant events of the past, from our current perspective. Our current perspective, however, changes constantly, as a result of political, social, and economic change.

We also asked the question, why learn about history? Self-evidently, we learn about history to know where we are, where we come from, and to consider where we are going. How the future will turn out depends on technological innovations, which may be part random, as well as individual actions, that too may be part random... History helps us understand a partially reconstructed past, as well as our present, but will always be a dialogue between present and past.

Appendix to Chapter 4: Doing history: the end of Japan's Pacific War

Noah McCormack

Source A) Henry Stimson, former U.S. Secretary of War, "The decision to use the atomic bomb", Harper's Magazine, February 1947.

The strategic plans of our armed forces for the defeat of Japan, as they stood in July, had been prepared without reliance upon the atomic bomb, which had not yet been tested in New Mexico. We were planning an intensified sea and air blockade, and greatly intensified strategic air bombing, through the summer and early fall, to be followed on November 1 by an invasion of the southern island of Kyushu. This would be followed in turn by an invasion of the main island of Honshu in the spring of 1946. The total U.S. military and naval force involved in this grand design was 5,000,000 men.

We estimated that if we should be forced to carry this plan to its conclusion, the major fighting would not end until the latter part of 1946, at the earliest. I was informed that such operations might be expected to cost over a million casualties, to American forces alone. Additional large losses might be expected among our allies, and, of course, if our campaign were successful and if we could judge by previous experience, enemy casualties would be much larger than our own.

- How does Stimson justify the decision to use the atomic bombs? Is his argument reasonable, or should we careful about some biases?

Source B) Harry S. Truman, U.S. President, Personal diary, 25 July 1945.

An experiment in the New Mexico desert was startling. Thirteen pounds of the explosive caused the complete disintegration of a steel tower 18m high, created a crater 1.8m deep and 365m in diameter, knocked over a steel tower 800m away and knocked men down 3km away. The explosion was visible for more than 320km and audible for 65km.

This weapon is to be used against Japan between now and August 10th. I have told the Sec[retary]. of War, Mr. [Henry] Stimson to use it so that military objectives and soldiers and sailors are the target and not women and children. Even if the Japs are savages, ruthless, merciless and fanatic, we as the leader of the world for the common welfare cannot drop this terrible bomb on the old Capitol [Kyoto] or the new [Tokyo].

He & I are in accord. The target will be a purely military one and we will issue a warning statement asking the Japs to surrender and save lives. I'm sure they will not do that, but we will have given them the chance. It is certainly a good thing for the world that Hitler's crowd or Stalin's did not discover the atomic bomb. It seems to me to be the most terrible thing ever discovered, but it can be made the most useful.

● What does Truman say about the use of the atomic bombs? What does he believe or assume? Is he correct in his assumptions? Is he an unbiased source?

Source C) The Potsdam Declaration

U.S. President Harry Truman, British Prime Minister Winston Churchill, and President Chiang Kai-shek of the Republic of China, 26 July 1945. (Joseph Stalin attends, but does not sign: Soviet entry into war is not until August 8 1945)

Para 3) The might that now converges on Japan is much greater than that which, when applied to the Nazis, necessarily laid waste to the lands, the industry, and the method of life of the whole German people. The full application of our military power backed by our resolve, will mean the inevitable and complete destruction of the Japanese armed forces and just as inevitably the utter devastation of the Japanese homeland.

Following are our terms. There are no alternatives.

We do not intend that the Japanese shall be enslaved as a race or destroyed as a nation, but stern justice shall be meted out to all war criminals.

The Japanese Government shall remove all obstacles to the revival and strengthening of democratic tendencies among the Japanese people. Freedom of speech, of religion, and of thought, as well as respect for the fundamental human rights shall be established.

The occupying forces of the Allies shall be withdrawn from Japan as soon as these objectives have been accomplished and there has been established in accordance with the freely expressed will of the Japanese people a peacefully inclined and responsible government.

We call upon the government of Japan to proclaim now the unconditional surrender of all Japanese armed forces, and to provide proper and adequate assurances of their good faith in such action. The alternative for Japan is prompt and utter destruction.

● What does the Potsdam declaration call for? Why? (What doesn't it call for, and why?) Consider what Truman writes in his diary: how does that help us (or not!) to understand this declaration?

Source D) Suzuki Kantarō, Prime Minister, responding to the Potsdam Declaration

[For] the enemy to say something like that means circumstances have arisen that force them also to end the war. That is why they are talking about unconditional surrender. Precisely at a time like this if we hold firm they will yield before we do. Just because they have broadcast their Declaration, it is not necessary to stop fighting. You advisers may ask me to reconsider but I don't think there is any need to stop [the war].

● What is Suzuki's interpretation of the Declaration? With the benefit of hindsight, was he correct? Is he affected by some kinds of biases?

Source E) Soviet Declaration of War on Japan, London, 8 August 1945

After the defeat and capitulation of Hitlerite Germany, Japan became the only great power that still stood for the continuation of the war.

The demand of the three powers, the United States, Great Britain and China, on July 26 for the unconditional surrender of the Japanese armed forces was rejected by Japan.

Taking into consideration the refusal of Japan to surrender, the Allies submitted to the Soviet Government a proposal to join the war against Japanese aggression and thus shorten the duration of the war, reduce the number of victims and facilitate the speedy restoration of universal peace.

Loyal to its Allied duty, the Soviet Government has accepted the proposals of the Allies and has joined in the declaration of the Allied powers of July 26.

The Soviet Government considers that this policy is the only means able to bring peace nearer, free the people from further sacrifice and suffering and give the Japanese people the possibility of avoiding the dangers and destruction suffered by Germany after her refusal to surrender.

In view of the above, the Soviet Government declares that from tomorrow, that is from Aug. 9, the Soviet Government will consider itself to be at war with Japan.

- How does the Soviet government explain its declaration of war on Japan? How do you think this logic looked to the Japanese government of the time? What biases might this source be affected by?

Source F) Japanese government top secret (ultra) message to government of Sweden, for transmission to governments of Britain, the United States, and the Soviet Union. 10.08.1945.

We have made the following decision. The Japanese government accepts the joint declaration decided upon in common by the leaders of the United States, Great Britain and China—in which declaration it later developed that the Soviet Union had had a part—on the condition that the stipulations of that declaration do not include any demand for alteration of the authority of the Emperor to rule the state.

- According to this, what is the primary or most important concern, from the point of view of the Japanese government?

Source G) Hirohito, Japanese monarch, Statement to Cabinet, 14 August 1945.

"Furthermore, it is fairly understandable to me that something like disarmament and military occupation is truly unbearable to the soldiers. But I would like to save my people's lives even at my expense. If we continue the war, the result will be that our homeland will be reduced to ashes. It is really intolerable for me to see my people suffering any more. I cannot be accountable to the spirit of our ancestors. If we choose peace, of course we cannot put our unconditional trust on the other side. But compared to the result of losing Japan itself we can at least hope for reconstruction as long as some seeds remain."

- What is Hirohito's conclusion? What is his stated reason for this conclusion? Can we trust what he says? What does he not say, that is significant?

1. *If we put these points together, what kind of multi-factor explanation for Japan's defeat in war starts to become visible?*
2. *What other factors that you are aware of led to the end of the Pacific War?*
3. *How are hindsight and post-facto clarity, topic choice bias, confirmation bias and national bias, issues in dealing with these kinds of sources?*
4. *Is it possible to say that any one factor was more important than the others (was decisive) in bringing about the end of World War II in the Pacific?*

Chapter 5 Ethics and morality

Masahiko Iguchi

Part 1. What is ethics?

Ethics is the academic name for the scientific study of morality. Morality refers to standards about good and bad, or right and wrong, that guide our decisions about how to act in various situations in society.

Is it alright to laugh at a sexist or racist joke told by a colleague or classmate? If your teacher mistakenly gives you very high grade, should you point out the mistake? In these cases, I think the answer is clear: It is not possible to say that enjoying sexist and racist jokes or benefiting from someone else's error are "good" actions. Sometimes, things are less obvious, however. Consider the following cases.

What would you do if you saw your best friend's lover kissing someone else? Would you be "honest" and tell your best friend about what you just saw? Or, would you not tell your best friend about it, assuming that it would damage your friend's relationship, in which, after all, you are not a participant?

Imagine you made a fairly serious mistake at your new part-time job: you mistook a thousand yen note that a customer handed you for a ten-thousand yen note and gave the customer 9,000 yen extra in change. The customer didn't say anything, left with the extra change, and haven't come back since. It turns out that your boss is blaming a veteran co-worker, who is known to often make mistakes. If you confess, you're likely to lose your job, which you are relying on. Should you confess, or stay silent?

Your country's government provides quite a lot of economic development assistance to another country that is geographically close, but much poorer than your own. However, the government of that country is involved in ethnic cleansing against an ethnic and religious minority. What should your country's government do? What should citizens, the media, and other parts of civil society in your country do?

Based on experience and convention, some of you may find it easy to give an opinion about what would be good or bad to do in each situation. Others may feel uncomfortable with having to choose a position to take. You may want to know more about the background and context of the events before making a decision, but it is possible to say that there are no simple and perfectly correct answers. Because it is hard to say what the right thing to do is in these cases, we call these kinds of situations **moral dilemmas**.

Academic studies of ethics

Convention or experience may be enough to deal with some moral dilemmas, but with more complicated issues, we may need some help from the academic field of ethics. Ethics can be roughly divided into three different specializations: Metaethics, Normative Ethics, and Applied Ethics. We won't spend too much time on these categories, but for reference, here is a quick outline.

Metaethics look at where our ideas about morality come from. For example, most people would agree with the statement that it is bad to kill human beings, including yourself, without extremely good justifications. But is it bad to kill because God said so (a reason from outside society), or because people in society collectively decided that it is bad (a reason based on society's collective rules), or because individuals' instincts or emotions or reason tells them that it is bad (a reason from within individual human beings)? By considering these kinds of questions, metaethics help us to think about whether our ideas about right and wrong, good and bad, virtuous and immoral, and so on are justified or reasonable.

Normative Ethics focuses on moral principles which we use to decide what is "right" to do or what is "wrong" to do. A famous example is the Golden Rule that says we should do to others what we would want others to do to us. These principles guide our actions. For example, if we accept the Golden Rule, then we can work out what we should do in many cases. If we would not want others to be rude or mean to us, then we should not be rude or mean to others. Likewise, if we would not want others to attack us, then we should not attack others. Thus, normative ethics tries to identify moral principles, and uses them to consider what we should do and what we should not do.

Finally, *Applied Ethics* seeks to clarify debates concerning particular issues that are controversial, such as "just war", "animal rights", "business ethics", and "medical ethics". The condition for a topic to be considered an issue of applied ethics is that there must be considerable disagreement over whether an act is moral or not. In these cases, it is obvious that there exists strong and considerable disagreement, for example, over whether war can ever be moral, whether animals can have rights and of what kind, whether anything goes in business or not, whether doctors should be allowed to help patients die in certain conditions, and so on. Applied ethics clarifies the arguments in contemporary moral arguments so that we can make better-informed judgements about how to act in cases of moral dilemmas.

Of course, these three fields are not always clearly separated from each other. Take the case of abortion. It involves questions of where rights come from (god or society or individuals?). It's also a normative issue, involving questions of who has the right to self-determination, as well as the right to life. Finally, it is also a morally controversial act that people strongly disagree about, so it is a matter for applied ethics too.

Activity: Thinking about abortion: the abstract and the personal

- *For you, in the abstract, is abortion "wrong", "acceptable", or "can't say"? Staying in the abstract, should women who become pregnant have the right to decide whether they will continue the pregnancy or not? What importance should the opinions of the father of the fetus have, in such a case? Is there any need to consider the possible intentions or desires of the fetus?*
- *Shifting to the concrete, imagine that you just found that you are pregnant, or that your partner is pregnant with your child. What would you do? Is abortion a possibility? What factors would you think about in making a decision? Next, think about the decision that you choose: what value or values is it based on? By choosing that or those particular values as most important, what values are you deciding to put less importance on?*

Thinking about these questions should help you see how it may be important for you personally to have some knowledge about applied ethics, normative ethics, and metaethics.

Activity: Personal and public ethics

- *In a group, choose one of the following topics, and prepare to give a short summary of ideas for and against the topic, using the chart below.*

A) *Should drugs such as heroin or cocaine be legalized?*

B) *Should hate-speech be protected as free speech?*

C) *Are small nuclear weapons "more evil" than larger conventional weapons?*

D) *Do citizens have a duty to make sacrifices for the state, for example, to fight in case of war?*

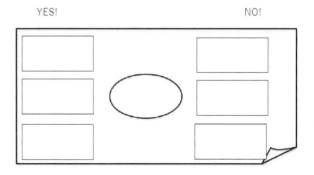

YES!　　　　　　　　　NO!

E)   *Should foreign aid be spent on projects that help those who most need aid wherever they are, or on projects that will be good for the national interest?*

F)   *If someone suffers from a serious and painful illness with no chance of recovery or improvement and wants to end his or her life but needs assistance to do so, should it be acceptable for a medical professional or other qualified person to help them die?*

Part 2. Moral reasoning

Although there are no straightforward answers to moral dilemmas (otherwise they wouldn't be dilemmas!), this doesn't mean that societies do not have broadly shared ideas about what is good and bad. In fact, a lot of our reasoning about morality is based on shared assumptions about right and wrong, which we can call **underlying or fundamental moral principles**.

One type of moral reasoning, which is based on such broadly shared moral principles, can be expressed in a form similar to the syllogisms used in deductive logic. It starts with a general statement—an underlying moral principle—like "murder is bad", and then applies it to a particular action: "Jill killed a stranger". Then, based on the first two statements, it arrives at a conclusion: "Jill acted wrongly", in this case. Often, we use this kind of reasoning without making the shared moral principles absolutely clear.

Activity: Identifying Moral Principles from Statements

●   *Re-write each of the statements below, to fit the format: 1. Underlying moral principle, 2. Particular case, 3. Conclusion based on 1 and 2.*

A)   *Example statement: Richard shouldn't have kept the money he found on the street.*
  1. *Moral principle: It is wrong to keep something you found that belongs to someone else.[43]*
  2. *Particular case: Richard found some money that someone dropped on the street, and he kept it.*
  3. *Conclusion: Richard was wrong to keep the money that he found.*

B)   *Paula cheated on a test, so she failed this class.*
  1) *Moral principle:*
  2) *Particular case:*
  3) *Conclusion:*

---

[43] Note that this norm is rather strong in Japan, but not so much in other places. There is an English saying, said to come from ancient Roman law, 'Finders keepers, losers weepers', which means that whoever finds something becomes its owner, while whoever lost that thing must suffer its loss! Morality varies a lot in time and place, and we shall see below.

C) *2. John shouldn't play his guitar until 2am in the morning.*
   1) *Moral principle:*
   2) *Particular case:*
   3) *Conclusion:*

D) *3. Connor should be released from prison since he didn't receive a fair trial.*
   1) *Moral principle:*
   2) *Particular case:*
   3) *Conclusion:*

E) *4. That politician lied to the parliament, so she should lose her position.*
   1) *Moral principle:*
   2) *Particular case:*
   3) *Conclusion:*

F) *5. That teacher was forced to resign after telling racist jokes in class.*
   1) *Moral principle:*
   2) *Particular case:*
   3) *Conclusion:*

Coherence, consistency, and truth

Assuming that we have underlying moral principles that we can all agree on, it is important that we use them *consistently*, and that when we use them to judge someone's actions, we are certain of the *truth* of the matter. Let's consider these two points in some more detail.

Consistency

Consistency requires that we treat all people who do the same thing in the same way. If it is wrong for Tom to cheat on the test, it must also be wrong for James and Harry to cheat on the test. This is because the same moral principle, in this case "you must not cheat on tests", must apply equally to everyone who cheats. If we make an exception for James and Harry, what happens? Well, obviously we would fall into the special pleading informal fallacy by giving James and Harry special consideration. This would constitute injustice to Tom, as well as to everyone else. But more significantly, our moral principles would fall into confusion. If it is wrong for some people to do something, but not for other people to do it, then the underlying moral principle is not really a moral principle, and we would not be able to use it to guide our actions. If morality's purpose is to help us to deal with complicated dilemmas in a rational way, consistency is absolutely necessary.

Unfortunately, people often hold inconsistent beliefs, apply their principles in inconsistent ways, or both. Take the idea that nuclear weapons are a bad thing because their use would involve massive and indiscriminate death and destruction. If enough people agreed with this idea, then it could become an underlying moral principle. If we accepted this principle, then to be consistent, we must agree that it is as bad for the U.S. to have nuclear weapons as it is for the Democratic People's Republic of Korea. However, in reality, people may think that U.S. nuclear weapons are not a major problem, whereas D.P.R.K. nuclear weapons are a major problem. If so, they would be showing moral inconsistency, in this case most likely as a result of holding emotional biases in favour of the U.S. and against the D.P.R.K.

Another common example of inconsistency concerns the killing of other human beings. Many people would agree with the general moral principle: "Killing people is wrong". Some people use that principle to argue against abortion, saying "It is wrong to kill an unborn child just because the parents do not want to have a child". But if those same people were to say that they support capital punishment because "All murderers should pay for their crime by losing their lives", then the two positions would not be logically consistent, because there is no doubt at all that capital punishment involves killing people. People may hold logically inconsistent positions in this case because they see the issues of abortion and capital punishment as being separate, but in fact, the same moral principle is involved.

Activity: Consistency

● *Identify the moral principle involved in each case, and judge whether the statements show any inconsistencies.*

Individual positions	Consistent/ inconsistent, and briefly explain why (moral principle)
Example: *Someone says it is wrong to steal, but often downloads movies and music from illegal websites.*	The underlying moral principle is, 'it is wrong to steal'. But illegal downloads constitute stealing. Inconsistent.
Someone is a vegetarian, and never wears animal fur coats or leather shoes.	
Someone claims to be an environmentalist but drives a super-charged sports car.	
Someone thinks state sovereignty is a key value, but says it is OK for the U.S. to have military bases in Japan.	

Truth

Truth is another important factor in deciding whether an action is good or bad. Before concluding that someone did X, which was a very good (or very bad) thing, it is obviously very important to check whether or not that actor actually did X or Y. Whether a politician is corrupt or a liar depends, first of all, on whether they actually took bribes, or whether they deliberately said things that were untrue. Before making the claim that Putin's government is bad because Russia interfered in the 2016 U.S. presidential elections, it is first necessary to check (a) whether Russia actually interfered in those elections, and (b) whether it was done on the orders of Putin's government. Without knowing the truth of the matter, we cannot make moral judgments about the Russian government's actions. Also, to be consistent, we would need to criticise U.S. government interference in the political affairs of many countries around the world in the post-war era.[44]

Sometimes, these questions can be solved by looking at empirical evidence. Imagine a weekly magazine published an article showing the following data: (a) Telephone records showing that Minister A, who was in charge of deciding which construction company would get a government contract to build certain sites for the Olympics, and construction company director B, who was in charge of a company that was bidding to get government contracts for Olympic site construction, talked on their mobile phones every day for several weeks before the winning bid was announced. (b) Bank data showing that during that time, a large amount of money was paid into A's bank account from B's wife's account. (c) An email from B to A saying "Thank you, again!" after B's company was announced as the winner of the government contract. It seems reasonable to conclude that these pieces of data establish or prove the fact of "corruption", and also suggests that the company director and the minister had engaged in other corrupt behaviour in the past as well. Knowing the 'truth' in this way, we might feel justified in making a moral decision that this politician did something "bad" (remembering to be consistent!).

However, the politician might claim that these pieces of information do not "prove" corruption. After all, bidding for government contracts is open and competitive. Company bids are examined by lots of bureaucrats and politicians, as well as the media. It is difficult, if not virtually impossible, for a single politician to choose a bid that is questionable. Imagine that B's company's bid was in fact proven to be the best bid, and A claimed the money was just a loan. In such a case, maybe

[44] See, for instance, Noam Chomsky, *Rogue states—the rule of force in world affairs*, Pluto Press, 2000, which examines U.S. unilateralism in the post-Cold War era, or his "The cognitive revolution", in *Language and politics,* AK Press, 2004, which touches on the post-WWII U.S. restoration of former fascist forces to power in Japan, Korea, Philippines, Indochina, and elsewhere.

we would have to change our mind about whether there was corruption or not. Probably we would still be able to say that the relationship between A and B looks unwise, but whether they did a bad thing would be uncertain, because the facts are ambiguous. What facts mean, in other words, is not always obvious. Knowing the truth is important, but what the truth *means* is often difficult to work out.

Activity: Determining relevant facts

● *What facts may be important in deciding about the morality of certain issues? That is, what would you need to know for sure, in order to answer yes or no to the following questions?*

Moral questions	Relevant facts to confirm
Example: *Should child labor be banned?*	- Is it necessary to survive? Do they have other options like school? - What are the working conditions? Are children exploited, abused, etc.? Is working clearly worse for children than not-working?
Should people under 18 years old be allowed to smoke cigarettes and drink alcohol?	
Should Genetically Modified foods be banned?	
Should rich countries should give more financial aid to poor countries?	

From the discussion above, it seems possible that morality is not too complicated, given the following conditions. (1) People share the same underlying moral principles. (2) People's judgments are consistent. (3) The facts can be made clear and easy to understand. However, these conditions are not often met in real life. In the real world, there is the problem of human inconsistency and irrationality: Many people judge using their emotions, rather than reason. Secondly, many "facts" are ambiguous: it is not possible to say precisely what they mean. These two problems are, in a sense, technical problems that can be solved by improving our reasoning skills and by engaging in dialogue to work out mutually accepted interpretations of "facts". However, there is a third and more important problem, which we turn to next: Different people hold different beliefs and values. In a world of diverse values and morality, is there any way to decide whose values and whose morality is "most correct"?

Part 3. Moral relativism

Different people have different morals. Morality can differ by country, religion, generation, by subculture even. If various groups in society each have their own sense of morality, is it possible to say that any group's morality is absolute? Maybe we should say that what is right or wrong depends on cultural and historical context? This kind of thinking is associated with moral relativism, which argues that morality is different for different groups of people in different places and times.

Consider that for people born in the mid-Showa period, sex before marriage was considered a bad thing. For people born during the late-Showa period, however, sex before marriage became quite a normal thing. Were the mid-Showa people "wrong"? Are the late-Showa and Heisei people "wrong"? If we take a moral relativist view, then we would say that both groups were correct, *for them*. If group X says premarital sex is bad, then it's bad *for them*. If group Y says premarital sex is not bad, then it's not bad for them. The relativist says that we cannot say any more than this. Let's take a few more examples.

In Verdi's opera, *Don Carlos*, the hero confesses his love for his step-mother, shocking the audience. But Verdi, remember, was writing for an Italian and European audience, which held Italian and European morality. If Don Carlos was held in Tibet, however, the shock might not arise. For in Tibet, for a father and son to share a single wife was not uncommon, historically. What is shocking for the Italians is not so for the Tibetans, and vice versa.[45]

The anthropologist Renato Rosaldo did fieldwork among the Ilongot peoples of the Philippines who were known once as head-hunters. Rosaldo was living with them during the time of the Vietnam War when he received notice of his likely conscription into the military from the U.S. government. When he explained the system of conscription to the Ilongot, they were horrified. Their horror was at the idea that someone would order others to do things they didn't want to do, and even more, that powerful people would order other people to go and fight on their behalf rather than go and fight themselves. Westerners might be horrified by headhunting and cannibalism, Rosaldo noted, but those headhunting cannibals are equally

---

[45] John W. Cook, *Morality and cultural differences,* Oxford University Press, 1999.

horrified by Western politicians' domination of other human beings, seeing this as highly immoral.[46]

Relativism and human diversity

People who take the moral relativist position may argue that human moral values are so diverse that there cannot be any objective and universal values. Humans have kept slaves, sacrificed people, mutilated their own and other people's sex organs, killed adulterers, burned widows, eaten people, and so on. Even if many people today think these things are dreadful, the people who did them didn't think they were wrong. (Their victims, of course, may have felt that these actions were very wrong!) But relativists suggest that human diversity indicates there is no ultimate basis for claiming that any one position is better than others.

Relativists would say that all morality is just a matter of social convention: a general agreement among people in society that they should act in a certain way in certain situations. For example, when driving in Japan, England and Australia, everybody agrees that they should drive on the left. This is a social convention: people agree to do it because they think it is in everyone's interest to do so. For relativists, morality is like this too. There is no deeper reason for the rule "do not kill" other than the fact that people agree that it is a good rule for them. But just as other people in different countries might decide that it is good to drive on the right side of the road, so might some people decide that it is acceptable for them not to have a "do not kill" rule.

Some philosophers think that morality is different to social convention because it has some kind of deeper meaning or justification. Consider the cases below and see what you think.

Activity: Morality and convention

- *Do you think the examples below are just conventions, like driving on the left side of the road, or are they deeper? As you go through these examples, can you find any pattern in your decisions?*

Examples	Morally wrong, or a matter of convention?
Example: Torturing innocent people.	A moral issue. Reason: Harming someone violates that person's human rights; harm without any good reason is even worse.

---

[46] Renato Rosaldo, *Culture & truth: the remaking of social analysis*, Beacon Press, 1993.

Male circumcision	
Female genital cutting	
Women with no make-up on.	
Men wearing high heeled shoes.	
One child pushes another off the swing.	
A student refuses to wear their school's uniform.	
Having more than one spouse (wives or husbands).	
Eating your healthy dog after it was killed by a passing car.	
Holding the door open for people coming after you.	
Neglecting a child so much that its development is affected.	
Placing the knife on the right and the fork on the left of your plate.	
Licking your plate at the table in a restaurant after you finish eating.	
Using people dead from natural causes, with permission obtained while they were alive, as resources (food, fertilizer, fuel).	

Lack of foundations for universal morality?

For relativists, there is no clear dividing line between social convention and morality, although some philosophers argue acts that cause pain and suffering are clearly immoral. However, the evidence for their arguments is not really sufficient for relativists, because morality doesn't seem to have any absolute or ultimate foundations. As the Scottish philosopher David Hume commented in the eighteenth century, we can gather facts about the world, and describe the world in terms of how it is. But from such knowledge, it is not possible to declare how we ought to live.[47]

---

[47] This is a problem of metaethics!

Morality may tell us what we should do. But whether it is justified in doing so is not at all clear. Consider this example, given in syllogism form.

A)   P1: *Some people in the world do not have enough money / food / clean water / education.*
B)   P2: *We have enough or more than we need of most of those things.*
C)   C1: *Therefore, we should give some of what we have to those who don't have enough.*

Emotionally, this argument may appear reasonable. But logically, the conclusion is not justified. The conclusion could just as well be one of the following.

A)   C2: *Therefore, we should thank God for looking after us.*
B)   C3: *Therefore, terrorists are always looking to attack us.*
C)   C4: *Therefore, we should all enjoy what we have been given.*

Only if we start by assuming a moral principle such as "Those who have enough should give some of what they have to those who do not have enough" can we reach C1 in a logical manner. The relativist perspective finds no reason for making this assumption, however, and concludes that moral relativism is the only justifiable position.

Against moral relativism

If relativism is the same as tolerance, then it may seem a quite attractive position. It stresses that we should "live and let live". After all, we don't like others telling us what values and beliefs we should hold, so why we should tell others how to live? But this kind of tolerance is not always possible. In particular, tolerant relativists face a dilemma when they meet members of an absolutist culture—a culture that is not tolerant or relativist but thinks that their cultures beliefs and practices are best. Say that this absolutist culture declares that the tolerant relativists have no right to exist because their beliefs are wrong. If the tolerant relativists accept that the intolerant culture's beliefs are as valid as their own, then how should they respond?

Relativism has been an important concept especially in anthropology, where is has helped to overcome ethnocentrism and racism. However, being relativist seems to involve a range of difficulties. If you treat all beliefs and values as equally valuable, then you can't resist the absolutists without betraying relativism. If you want to resist, and think the absolutists should become tolerant,

Ethnocentrism

Evaluating other cultures based on the standards and customs of your own culture. Strictly speaking, the Ilongot critique of Western conscription is a form of ethnocentrism, as is the Western critique of Ilongot head-hunting!

then you end up proposing tolerance as a universal value. Then, you're no longer a consistent moral relativist. Viewed like this, moral relativism may lose its appeal, especially since it offers no protection against imperialists, absolutists, dictators, mass murderers, and so on.

Relativism and globalization

Human life everywhere is quite similar, as it depends on cooperation to meet similar needs and overcome similar problems. Because of this, human societies always come up with similar rules that enable living with others, limit violence, protect property, and promote honesty. In order to flourish, a society needs to be fundamentally just. However, historically, societies have not needed to cooperate with outsiders in order to flourish, and because of this, they have rarely been considerate of non-members.

In today's global system, we are possibly moving beyond in-group bias, recognizing our common humanity, and developing a shared set of values. Associations such as Amnesty International propose that there are universal standards of human rights, which everybody should enjoy. The United Nations Declaration of Human Rights also assumes that there are shared universal moral standards. This kind of universalism proposes that rules and standards exist, independent of our personal preferences.

Activity: Morality, relativism, and globalization

- *What effects do you think globalization will have on moral relativism? Is it likely to get stronger or weaker? Why? What kinds of examples are suitable for discussing these questions?*
- *What effects did the encounter between 19th century Euro-America and Japan lead to, in terms of morality? Consider examples like: buying and selling people, killing people, nudity, mixed bathing, and so on. Is the same kind of convergence happening on a global scale today?*

Selfish human nature as a problem for universal morality

Actually, some people think that any attempt to set out universal human morality is doomed, because they think humans are innately selfish. In their view, we think that what is good for us is moral, and what is bad for us is immoral. If this is true, then it would seriously limit the possibility of any shared or common morality, so next let us briefly consider the main points of this argument.

One argument says that we are selfish when we do what we want to do. Since everyone wants to do what they want to do, and most of us are successful at least some of the time in doing so, it's possible to say that humans are all selfish. But this definition of selfishness seems to be rather problematic. It implies that Donald Trump, who is a multi-billionaire devoted to seeking more money and more power, and Mother Teresa, who devoted herself to helping others, are equally selfish, because both are just doing what they want to do. Can we agree with this? Probably not. Surely there is an important difference between self-regarding desires (desires only for yourself) and other-regarding desires (desires to help other people). The existence of other-regarding desires suggests that humans are not purely selfish.

A second argument says that humans are biologically programmed to be selfish, to ensure their own survival and that of their children. This may be true. But human societies have been successful at least partly because people are very good at working with others. Empathy, helpfulness, and cooperation have been universal features of human society, and these do not seem to be a good fit for the idea that humans are fundamentally self-interested and selfish. In fact, many psychologists believe that humans are pro-social. Studies of even very small babies suggest that we naturally empathize with others and like to help them.[48] This argument too, does not seem to disallow the possibility of universal moral standards.

A third argument says that even acts that help others are selfish, because the person who does them benefits in various ways. For example, the 17th-century philosopher Thomas Hobbes once gave money to a beggar. Because Hobbes was well-known for arguing that humans always act out of self-interest, someone asked him why he did this. Hobbes answered that the beggar's desperate situation made him feel bad, so he was trying to make himself feel less bad by giving the beggar some money. It was a self-interested act of giving.

However, getting benefits is not the only reason that we do good things. Cases in which people help others they have no need to help at great personal risk suggest a strong human concern with justice and fairness, beyond self-interest. Chiune Sugihara, a Japanese diplomat who served as consul for the Japanese Empire in Lithuania, is famous for his moral actions. During the Second World War, he helped thousands of Jewish people to escape from Europe by issuing transit visas to them, risking his job and his family's lives. The fact that it is common to donate aid to far-away people faced with disaster also suggests that humans have an altruistic side, and that universal morality is a possibility. Overall, it seems possible to say that we are not entirely selfish, even if we are not always altruistic either.

---

[48] See, for example, Martin L. Hoffman, *Empathy and moral development*, Cambridge University Press, 2000.

Activity: Thinking about doing good

A) If you helped someone, and they weren't grateful, what would you think?
B) If you gave a lot of money to charity, would you want your friends to know about it?
C) If you once helped someone, but they didn't help you when you needed help, how would you feel?
D) Do you think you are more likely to help someone in trouble if there are other people watching, or if there is no-one else around?
E) Even if you were all-powerful and at no risk of being punished, do you think there are still likely to be things that you wouldn't do?

Examples of altruistic behaviour?

At the National Prayer Breakfast, President Obama told the story of a group of Americans who were captured by the Nazis during World War II. The head of the German prison camp gave an order that the Jewish soldiers step forward. An American master sergeant, Roddie Edmonds, ordered all of his men to step forward. The Nazi held a gun to the sergeant's head and said, "These can't all be Jewish." The sergeant replied, "We are all Jews." Rather than execute all of the men, the Nazi backed down.

In Larissa MacFarquhar's recent book, "Strangers Drowning," she writes about radical do-gooders. One of her subjects started a leper colony in India. One couple had two biological children and then adopted 20 more kids who needed a home. A woman risked rape to serve as a nurse in wartorn Nicaragua. One couple lived on $12,000 a year so they could donate the additional money they earned annually, about $50,000, to charity. One abandoned a marriage to serve the poor. These people were often driven by moral rage and a need to be of pure service to the world. They tend to despise comfort and require a life that is difficult, ascetic and self-sacrificial. They yearn for the feeling that they are doing their utmost to relieve suffering.

From: David Brooks, "A Question of Moral Radicalism", *The New York Times*, 05.02.2016.

Part 4. Ethical frameworks

Moral diversity does not necessarily mean relativism is the answer, especially in a globally connected age of mass travel and migration. Nor does human selfishness disallow moral behaviour and knowledge. But where can we find a solid foundation for universal human morality?

Some may suggest that *emotions* provide a basis for morality: we empathize with other people's pain, and indeed with the pain of animals too, and so minimizing pain of all animals that can feel pain could be an important moral principle. However, the problem here is that not everyone feels the same emotions. Indeed, some people known as sadists enjoy seeing the pain other others, while masochists enjoy their own pain. Further, our emotions are quite inconstant—they change all the time. Thus, emotion doesn't seem like a very good basis for ethics. The same goes for *intuition*.

Historically, *religions* provided rules and guidance about how to live. But the variety of religious texts presents us with the problem of which to choose: Is there a "correct" text, or are they all correct in their own war? It doesn't look like there are any rational grounds for choosing, say, the Koran or the Bible above Buddhist or Hindu texts.

Secondly, there are problems involving language. Many religions are based on modern translations of ancient texts: Are the translations correct? After the September 11, 2001 suicide bombings in the United States, many media mentioned how the Koran promises martyrs who die for Islamic causes a range of rewards, including 72 "virgins" for their post-death pleasure. Leaving aside the problem of such a sexist vision of paradise, Christoph Luxenberg has recently written that actually, a lot of the Koran has been mistranslated. Many words thought to have been Arabic were in fact Syriac, and the "virgins" were actually white raisins: martyrs were to be served cold grape drinks, probably. Thus, Islamic suicide bombers who imagine that they will be going to a paradise with lots of women to serve them are, from this point of view, acting based on a mistaken belief that originates in mistranslation.[49] If this kind of problem is common in religious texts, it seems to be rather risky to depend on them to be our guides to morality.

Further, texts like the Christian Bible are internally contradictory because they were written by different people at different times from different perspectives. Some parts of the Christian Old Testament state that "God is a vengeful god", "a warrior […] a consuming flame", angry, fierce, jealous, furious and so on. This Old Testament god is a frightening, angry, murderous figure. But the New Testament god is quite different: "God is love", "love, job, peace, patience, kindness, goodness, faithfulness, gentleness, and self-control". If you focus on the Old Testament, then Christianity feels like a fighting and revenge-focused religion. If you focus on the New Testament, then Christianity becomes a much warmer and softer religion. Texts that contain such diversity are not suitable as guides to universal morality because they can be used to justify anything from universal love to wars of revenge and punishment. The situation becomes even more complicated if we consider that interpretations of those ancient ideas translated into modern languages are extremely diverse. Overall, it seems quite clear that religious texts are unlikely to give us a reliable guide to how to live our lives and deal with contemporary moral dilemmas. Given the disagreements between as well as within religious institutions, it is

---

[49] Christoph Luxenberg, *The Syro-Aramaic reading of the Koran*, Schiler, 2007.

unlikely that any universal moral guidance can be expected from them either. Perhaps philosophy and *reason* can provide us with somewhat better guidance.

Kantian ethics

According to the great German philosopher Immanuel Kant, ethics is fundamentally a matter of doing your duty and fulfilling your obligations. Being ethical is all about doing what you have to do. What are our duties? Kant suggested that it is possible to work out what duties we have using reason.

Activity: Thinking about duty

● *Say you're in a hurry to get to your part-time job after class, but there is a long line for the bus. It's so long that it looks like you might have to wait for the next bus, and then you might be late for work. Should you stand in line? Would it be permissible to cut into the queue so that you can get on the bus?*

Kant says that we should do our duty. What would our duty be in this case? To decide what our duty is in a certain situation, Kant suggested that we should ask whether an action can be consistently generalized. He meant that when we choose a course of action, we should do things that we would want everyone to do (this is his Categorical Imperative). Before cutting into the line for the bus, we should ask: Would it be reasonable to want everyone to do it? If we cannot answer "Yes", it is our duty not to do it. In this case, would we want everyone to ignore the queue? Well, probably not: getting on the bus would become a chaotic struggle, with the strongest and most violent getting on first. It's unlikely that we would welcome this. So, it is our duty not to cut into the queue.

Activity: Generalization and duty

● *Decide whether the following are duties or not, by generalizing them. In other words, consider what would happen if everyone did it?*

Actions	What would happen, if everyone does that?
Example: Not paying taxes	If no one pays taxes, then, there would be no revenue for the government, no social services, and a lot of chaos and uncertainty. So, it is our duty to pay taxes.
Breaking promises	
Not voting in elections	
Leaving garbage in the park	
Skipping classes	
Answering job interview questions truthfully	

Committing suicide	

Impartiality and respect for individuals

Kant's Categorical Imperative—working out what our duty is by asking if we can universalize an action or not—also eliminates the possibility of special pleading. Human beings often engage in special pleading—saying we should be allowed some special privilege or exemption from an obligation that others do not have—because we think that we are special, or that our friends and family are special. And this is partly true: each individual is very special for that individual. We each only have one "me", and this is one of the most valuable things that we have. But Kant said that we need to be careful not to focus too much on our individual "me", and remember that every individual, including but not limited to our own self, is a "me", and so we are all "one me among others". In other words, because everyone is a "me", being a "me" cannot justify special treatment.

In order to help us overcome our tendency to engage in special pleading and to achieve greater impartiality, philosophers such as John Rawls suggest that we should try to think using a **veil of ignorance**.[50] For example, we could try to imagine how society or politics should be re-arranged to achieve a fairer or more just society, on the assumption that we do not know the position that we would hold in the new arrangements. A simple example concerns the division of a single cake between two people. Say the person who cuts it gets to choose which piece they will have. In such a case, they have an incentive to make one piece bigger than the other (if they like cake!), so the result risks being unfair. But if one person cuts and the other person chooses, then the cutter has an interest in making the cut as even or as fair as possible, because the cutter doesn't know which piece they will get. Rawls' idea is that this principle can help us design political, social and economic arrangements not from our own interested or selfish perspective (the standpoint of the "me"), but more from an impartial perspective that sees us as "one among others".

The dignity of humans

Even as Kant stated that we should think of ourselves as one among others to avoid giving any individual special treatment, he also pointed out that no individuals should be discriminated against either, because each person is also an individual me.

---

[50] John Rawls, *A theory of justice*, Harvard University Press, Rev. Ed. 1999.

Each me has only one life and must not be treated as a means to an end or a tool. The reason for this was Kant's view that humans had dignity.

Kant contrasted the idea of dignity with the idea of value. He proposed that objects can have value. But value is subjective, because something's value depends on the observer's viewpoint. What is valuable for me may not be for you. Further, things that have value can be replaced by something else of equal value. However, he thought people were special. With the power to reason, and to live life freely and morally, humans have to be respected for what they are: autonomous rational beings. Because of this, he reasoned that humans had dignity, which is irreplaceable, and much greater than value.[51] Because dignity is equal, individual and irreplaceable, an individual person should never be sacrificed for any larger purposes. However, things with value might be sacrificed as a means to achieve some purpose.

Activity: People are not things

- *Brainstorming: how are people (friends, family, acquaintances) different from things (jewelry, watches, computers)? Explain with examples.*
- *How do Kant's ideas fit with, for example, conscription (compulsory military service), and fighting in a war, or with so-called "black companies"?*

Kant also argued that the moral value of actions depends on the motivation of actors, rather than the action's consequences. Doing something because you expect a reward of some kind would not be a good motivation. For example, being nice to small children because someone whose opinion you care about is watching would not be a praiseworthy motivation. Doing something because of the way you feel, for Kant, was also not a particular good thing. Helping someone because they are cute or good-looking would be an example of this. On a larger scale, following this same logic, giving foreign aid to a particular country in the hope of receiving future economic benefits would not be an ethical action, and nor would giving aid to the victims of humanitarian disasters because of sympathy for their difficult situation. Obviously, performing capital punishment or going to war because of anger or resentment or for revenge would also be wrongly-motivated acts. Kant believed that the only moral motivation for action was duty, based on reason. We should do things because our reason tells us it is our duty to do them, rather than because we want to benefit from doing so, or because of the very changeable way that we feel.

Activity: Good acts and good motivations

- *Rank the following in terms of bad, worse, worst. Explain your reasoning. What do you think Kant would say about the two examples?*
- A) *X kills Y on purpose.*

---

[51] Oliver Sensen, *Kant on human dignity*, de Gruyter, 2011.

B)   A kills B and C by mistake.
C)   D plans to kill E, but fails.

- *From Kant's point of view, who is doing their duty, or acting with good motivations? What do you think about his thinking?*
A)   Someone who helps another person because s/he likes that person.
B)   Someone who helps another person even though s/he doesn't like them.

Problems with Kantian ethics

To actually live by Kantian ethics seems rather difficult. For a start, he proposes that we shouldn't do things because of the way we feel or because of what we want, but because of our duty. To know our duty, we must use *reason*. But not all of us are equally good at using our reason. Not only that, but to think about the question, "What if everyone did it", we also need a considerable amount of *imagination* too. Further, it often happens that our *emotions* are stronger than our reason, so that even if we know what our duty is, our emotions may stop us from doing it.

Also, Kantian ethics propose rules that are absolute. We are to work out our duty by reasoning in terms of universals: If we would not want everyone to lie, disobey speed limits when driving, or rebel against the government, then to live according to Kantian ethics, we should never lie, disobey speed limits, rebel against the government, and so on. Can you agree with this idea? Can you live with such an absolute set of rules?

Activity: Exceptions to rules

A)   When is it acceptable or good to lie?
B)   When do you think it is acceptable or good to disobey speed limits and other traffic rules?
C)   When do you think it is acceptable or good to rebel against a government?
D)   When is it acceptable or good to kill a human being?

Finally, critics have pointed out that Kantian ethics has a problem with duties that conflict with other duties. When this happens, it is not clear which duty we should choose. For example, one rule might be that it is wrong to steal. Another rule might be that parents should look after their children. If you had a child who was dying of a rare disease, and you didn't have enough money to pay for the very expensive operation that would be necessary to treat the disease, would you be justified in stealing to get the money? Kantian ethics provides no easy way to make a decision in moral dilemmas like this one that involve duty conflicts.

Activity: Duty conflict

- *What moral principles are in conflict in the examples below? Choose one and explain why it should be resolved in a particular way.*

Cases	Choices	Reason
Example: *You have been unfaithful to a lover.*	A) Be honest and tell the truth. B) Say nothing / lie.	In general, telling the truth is the right thing to do, and lying is not. However, making your lover unhappy may not seem like the right thing to do…
1. On a sinking ship, there's only one seat available in a life raft, which you can give to your mother, or to a famous brain surgeon.	A) Your mother. B) The brain surgeon.	
2. A terrorist group kidnaps a group of students and threatens to kill them unless the government pays a lot of money and releases a group of imprisoned terrorists.	A) Refuse their demands. B) Meet their demands.	

Utilitarianism

In this section, we explore some of the good points and weak points of utilitarianism, a theory of ethics that appears to be quite different to Kantian ethics. The main idea of utilitarianism is that morally right actions are those that produce the most good. In contrast to Kant, who stressed universal rules and duty as conditions for moral action, utilitarians consider the consequences of an action to decide whether that action is moral or "good". A good action, for a utilitarian, is one that increases the amount of happiness in the world or decreases the amount of unhappiness in the world. Doing whatever will help achieve the greatest possible amount of happiness for the most people possible is a good thing.

Activity: Utilitarianism in everyday life

- *Marie Kondo (of the Kon-Mari Method) achieved global fame through her suggestion for organizing your possessions by dividing them into things that "spark joy", and those that don't. Does this sound like a utilitarian philosophy for everyday living?*
- *What kinds of changes would utilitarianism lead to in your everyday life?*

How would we decide what increases happiness in the world? Jeremy Bentham, an important utilitarian thinker, proposed that when we have to make a decision about how to act, we should try to calculate the total amounts of pleasure and pain that would result, and perform a kind of cost-benefit assessment. Say you have promised to have dinner this coming Friday with your grandparents who are traveling a long distance to meet you. Say, also, that someone in whom you have long had a romantic interest has invited you to dinner this coming Friday. Unless you want to have a combined dinner (which might be fun!?), you are going to have to disappoint someone. Who should you disappoint? Bentham suggested we should think about seven criteria when we try and work out what to do.

Table 12 Bentham's criteria for measuring pleasure and pain

Intensity	How strong the pleasure or pain is.
Duration	How long the pleasure or pain lasts.
Probability	How certain it is that pleasure or pain will be caused.
Timing	How close or far the action and the pleasure or pain are in time.
Prospects	How likely it is that the act will lead also to future pleasures and pains.
Purity	How much other sensations are mixed in with pleasure and pain.
Extent	How many people would be affected.

The difficulty of utilitarian thinking

You'd need to spend quite some time thinking about most situations in order to make a decision! Actually, one criticism of Bentham's utilitarianism has focused on this point: It's too complicated, and so it's not realistic to expect people to actually think like this in everyday situations. When it comes to decisions about how to allocate government spending, on military equipment and weapons or on public education and healthcare, for example, or whether to go to war or not, the calculations are likely to become tremendously complicated—so much so that they may be beyond human abilities to calculate. Artificial intelligence may be able to help us in these calculations in the relatively near future, however.

Activity: Gross National Happiness

● *Many countries have a measure of Gross National Happiness today. Research how they calculate this, and consider how well, or not, they meet Bentham's seven criteria.*

Activity: Applying Bentham's criteria

● *Use Bentham's seven criteria to consider the following acts in terms of pleasure and pain*
A) *Playing video games all night.*
B) *Finishing a difficult and lengthy essay.*
C) *Smoking a packet of cigarettes every day for ten years.*
D) *Dating someone for whom your feelings are not very strong.*
E) *Working in a series of unstable but enjoyable jobs at average pay.*
F) *Eating a whole box of chocolates by yourself while watching a movie.*
G) *Working all your life in a job that you don't like but which has a decent salary and work environment.*

Activity: The trolley problem

- *You are a bystander seeing a runaway trolley, about to hit and kill five people. You can control a switch and reroute it to a different track where it will kill only one person. Should you?*

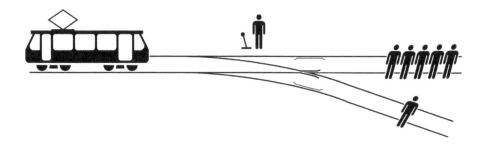

Figure 7 The Trolley Problem

Issues with utilitarianism

Apart from complexity, another major criticism of utilitarianism is that pleasure is not the only thing that we care about. Indeed, pleasure may not even be the most important thing in life for many people. Some people put freedom above everything, others put the welfare of other people first, while still others value the truth, even if it doesn't make them happy, above anything else.

Additionally, it is difficult to measure and compare pleasure with any accuracy. Consider that you and your friend are the two final candidates for a single position with a famous company. Getting the job would make you happy and make you friend unhappy. Your friend getting the job would make your friend happy and make you unhappy. But how would you measure your happiness or unhappiness, and how could you compare it with your friend's happiness or unhappiness?

A further problem is that we don't know the consequences of our actions ahead of time, largely because who we are in the present is not who we will be in the future. Sometimes, we imagine that getting something will cause us a lot of happiness. Maybe you imagine that getting a job with a well-known company will make you happy, or that getting married or having children will make you happy. But if you achieve those things, you may not be as happy as you expected, because at that stage, you will no longer be the person you used to be. You will be someone with a job, or a spouse, or children. And so naturally, the things that will make you happy will be different too.[52] In short, using expected or predicted consequences to guide our actions may be a very unreliable way of proceeding.

Finally, focusing on consequences more than motivations may encourage people to think that the ends justify the means. To take a rather extreme example, let's say someone invented a new drug, with no side-effects, that makes people feel happy. People can do their jobs and study and live regular lives as usual, except that they are permanently happy. Clearly, a strict utilitarian viewpoint may consider that it is a good thing, to give this drug to everybody. Then we would massively increase the world's total amount of happiness without causing any pain. Would this be a truly good thing to do? What do you think? Many people think it wouldn't be good, because it would be a kind of "empty pleasure".

Activity: Is lack a condition for happiness?

- *You can't be happy unless you lack something, said Bertrand Russell. Considering the last paragraph, can you explain what he meant? Do you agree?*

Activity: What is happiness?

A) *Are rich people with lots of free time happy? Are poor and hungry people universally less happy than wealthier well-fed people? Would redistribution of money from rich to poor increase or decrease the total amount of happiness?*

B) *Which is preferable: a situation in which you earn 5 million yen a year and your friends all earn 2.5 million yen, or a world in which you earn 10 million yen a year, and your friends all earn 25 million yen a year? What is the significance of your answer for utilitarianism?*

C) *You're having dinner at a friend's house and the food is awful—asked how the meal is, how do you answer? How should you answer?*

D) *An elderly man is in hospital for a health check. He has few friends, no relatives, is disliked by most people, and doesn't seem to enjoy life, but is in very good health. Many patients in the hospital need organ transplants, and the elderly man is a perfect match in terms of blood type: his body could provide life and happiness for at least 10 patients, and all their family and friends. Should he be killed?*

E) *There is a child-abusing violent unpleasant woman in the neighborhood. Should someone get rid of her?*

A clarification on utilitarian thinking

Actually, returning to the criticism that utilitarianism may justify ends over means, it is not clear that it could actually justify sacrificing individuals for the greater good. Proper use of Bentham's criteria would probably make this highly unlikely. In reality, if we killed someone for body parts or to get rid of someone unpleasant, we would feel guilty. Not only that, but such killings would be bad from

---

[52] On this, check out Slavoj Žižek's *Trouble in paradise*, Allen Lane, 2014.

a utilitarian perspective, because random killings would cause general fear and terror, and lower everyone's happiness levels. Utilitarian thinkers would probably agree that people's individual rights should be protected, because that will help raise everyone's happiness levels! On this point, utilitarianism seems to approach Kantian ethics, which would also agree that it is good (our duty) to respect individual rights. This leads us to our final topic in this chapter.

Rule utilitarianism

In Kantian ethics and utilitarianism, we have two very different guidelines for moral action. One stresses absolute rules and duty as the only good motivation. The other stresses pleasure over pain, and suggests ends are more important than means and motivations. Both frameworks seem valuable, but they appear quite far apart in their recommendations. Must we choose one over the other?

Rule utilitarians believe that the two types of moral guidelines can be combined. To do this, they propose that we should focus not on individual acts, but rather on general rules informed by experience about how to act. The past provides us with a guide to the rules that usually help to promote general happiness.

For example, experience may show that happiness levels are generally higher for university graduates compared to junior high school graduates. If so, then utilitarianism would say that it is, generally speaking, good to go to university and graduate. However, rule utilitarianism includes an extra step. Even if we have a rule that leads to general happiness ("Go to university!"), when we consider a particular case or moral dilemma, we should think about whether following the rule will bring about more good than bad, or more happiness than unhappiness *in that case*. Thus, while it may be generally good to go to university and graduate, for particular people, being in a classroom and having to write essays and sit exams may feel like unbearable torture. Thus, for those people, rule utilitarians would say, going to university may cause them more pain than pleasure, so they should not have to go to university.

To take another example, we know from experience that it is good to stop at red traffic lights. This helps us avoid accidents, and so reduces unhappiness in the world. However, there may be times when stopping at a red traffic light could increase the total amount of unhappiness in the world. At such times, we would be justified in not stopping. What kinds of situations are we talking about? Well, if there are no cars in sight, and you have a pregnant woman in the car who is about to give birth, and you need to get to a hospital in a hurry, then ignoring the red light will probably help increase your levels of happiness and decrease your levels of unhappiness. Another eminent utilitarian, John Stuart Mill, argued this point in his book *Utilitarianism*. It may not only be justified, but in fact your duty to break rules if it is to save a life or prevent great harm.

The basic framework of rule utilitarianism can be summarized as follows. You should keep to rules that experience tells us are good for general happiness. "However, if there are good reasons for not following those rules in particular cases, you may be justified in breaking those rules." There is, however, quite some debate about what kinds of exceptions are acceptable.

Activity: Thinking with the frameworks

● *Which do you think is worse: being rude and unkind to someone, or saying rude and unkind things about someone behind their back and being polite to their face? Do Kantian ethics, utilitarianism, or rule utilitarianism help us to answer this?*

Conclusion

In this chapter, we have looked at ethics from a range of perspectives. Firstly, we considered the academic discipline of ethics as the study of morality, and the different areas that are included within this discipline. Ethics includes the study of where our morals come from, what they mean in our everyday lives, and how they are used in controversial debates.

Secondly, we looked at how everyday knowledge is often used to make moral judgements, even though our common sense and moral reasoning are often not founded on reason. Because of this, moral diversity and moral relativism may seem at first glance as though they are good positions to take. However, we suggest that moral relativism is a dangerous position to take, and that in fact, in the context of globalization and communication across borders, and the development of norms about universal human rights, we are currently moving towards a world in which morality is becoming widely shared.

Thirdly, we also looked at the argument that people are selfish, and so cannot be expected to engage in moral behaviour. However, our consideration of this argument suggests that humans are not only selfish, but are also social, cooperative, and frequently concerned with the welfare of others. These points indicate that it is reasonable to expect moral behaviour of others.

Finally, in the most philosophical section of the chapter, we looked at Kantian ethics, utilitarianism, and rule utilitarianism, to consider different reason-based moral frameworks for action. Introducing an approach that emphasizes duty, an approach that emphasizes happiness, and an approach that attempts to synthesize or combine the two, we hope that we have provided you with ideas that will stimulate you to do some independent research regarding ethics, and also knowledge that will help you make better decisions in your life!

Chapter 6 The Arts

Russell Garofalo

Art is a lie that brings us nearer to the truth.
Picasso.

Part 1. Ubiquitous art

Before we begin this chapter, please take a moment to look around you. Look at the objects on your desk. Look at the bag you brought with you today. Look at your clothes. Now look at your teacher and your classmates and all the things they have with them. Finally, look at the room you are sitting in and all the furniture in it. Although there may be no copy of the Mona Lisa (by Leonardo da Vinci) or Starry Night (by Vincent Van Gogh) hanging from the walls in your classroom, art and design are everywhere. Somebody designed this classroom, these desks, your shoes, your bag, and your smart phone. When we talk about art and design, we are referring to all the things around us that have been imagined, planned, and produced by human beings. We may divide these items into different categories. Here are some of them:

A) Fashion
B) Interior design
C) Technological design
D) Graphic design
E) Product design
F) Architecture
G) Packaging
H) Advertising
I) Painting
J) Literature
K) Photography
L) Music
M) Illustration
N) Sculpture
O) Film

Activity: Describing art

- *For each of the categories of art and design above, list at least one example, and if possible, describe it a little. (It should be mentioned here that some of these categories overlap with others. For example, an advertisement for Coca-Cola includes graphic design, product design, and packaging design.) Here are some other examples to get you started:*

A) An example of fashion is a jacket with The North Face logo on it.
B) Examples of interior design are the cushioned chairs in this classroom.
C) Technological design includes a Sony TV.
D) Graphic design includes a pamphlet a student handed me this morning as I walked up the hill to class. It had a cartoon and an announcement on it.
E) An example of product design is the pen or pencil that are you using right now.
F) Architecture includes the Tokyo Tower.
G) Packaging includes the lettering and coloring on the package of a Snickers bar.
H) An example of advertising art is the logo and slogan for Nike: "Just do it."
I) Painting includes Pablo Picasso's *Guernica*.
J) Literature includes Nobel Prize winner Kazuo Ishiguro's novel *The Remains of the Day*.
K) Photography includes the portrait of John Lennon and Yoko Ono taken on the afternoon of John Lennon's death by photographer Annie Leibovitz.
L) Music includes Beethoven's *5th Symphony.*
M) Illustration includes comic books like *OnePiece*.
N) One of the most famous sculptures is Auguste Rodin's *The Thinker*.
O) Film includes the *Star Wars* movies.

After making your lists and sharing them with others in your class, hopefully it has become clear that art is everywhere. Thus, to be in the world means to be looking at, wearing, sitting on, standing in, using, and listening to "art".

In today's world, we honour great interior designers like the Brazilian designer Sergio Rodrigues who was famous for designing chairs, or great fashion designers like the French designer Christian Dior who was most famous for designing women's clothing. In 2017, the Christian Dior company had an exhibition in Paris, which included the different dresses and outfits designed every year for the past 70 years. This exhibition attracted thousands of people who came just to see the dresses that were made from the past until today. None of the dresses was on sale. Thus, fashion, while having a practical function, can also be viewed simply as "art for art's sake". "Art for art's sake" means to enjoy art just for its beauty, not for any practical, symbolic, or philosophical purpose.

However, not everyone agrees that everything that has been designed is art. Some things may be simply a functional item like a park bench, or a practical item like a tube of toothpaste. Although somebody designed them, their main purpose is to be used, not to be enjoyed as art.

Activity: Art and not-art

A) *Look at the categories of different kinds of art and design again (letters a-n above). Which kind of art and design is pure art? That means it only exists as art and has no other purpose. Explain your answers.*
B) *Which kind of art and design should not be considered art at all, and is really just a functional item? Explain your answers.*
C) *Which kind of art and design can be considered both pure art and a practical item? Explain your answers.*
D) *In your opinion, is there is a difference between "pure art" and "practical or consumer items"? What is the difference?*

Indeed, it has become commonplace in today's world to consider nearly anything as an "art". There is the art of cooking, the art of playing chess, and even the art of conversation. In a sense, "art" simply means anything done mindfully, with some creativity, and with a particular method.

Activity: Defining art

A) *Do you think cooking is an art? Why or why not?*
B) *What are the martial arts? Make a list of all the ones you can think of.*
C) *Should the martial arts be considered "art"? Aren't martial arts like karate more like a sport or a game? In what way are they "art"?*
D) *Is playing baseball an "art"? When can it be considered an art, and when can it be considered a sport? Are all sports "art"?*
E) *Should Western chess, Japanese shogi, or go be considered arts, or are they simply games? What is the difference between an art and a game?*
F) *What other activities or things can be considered art? Try to think of things not mentioned already in this chapter and explain why you think so.*

As you can see, defining "art" is not easy. In some ways, everything is art. And yet, there are some things specifically made as "pure art" or what we call "fine art". Let's now turn our attention to the pure art object.

Definition of fine art

First, it will be helpful to have a definition of fine art. Fine art means a work that is meant to be enjoyed solely for its aesthetic value. That is, its only purpose or value is as a work of imagination, beauty, and creativity. It has no other value or purpose except for "being art" and is not meant to be used in any way. It is simply meant to be seen, or heard, and to have some mental impact on the viewer. Thus, Michelangelo's sculpture David is fine art. You are meant to look at it and appreciate its beauty. On the other hand, Steve Jobs's iPhone is not fine art. Although it is beautiful, and can be considered a kind of minimalist art, you are meant to use it. It is therefore considered industrial or technological design rather than art.

Fine art traditionally includes painting, sculpture, music, architecture, and literature. There are also the performing fine arts such as theatre, like a Shakespeare play, and dance, like ballet. More recently, we include design, film, and photography, among others, as fine art. However, for our purposes in this chapter, let us limit our discussion to the traditional fine arts, and specifically the visual arts like painting and sculpture.

Chances are that even if you think you don't know much about fine art, you probably have seen more famous artworks than you think. This is because famous artworks are part of our worldwide human culture. Western artists like Leonardo da Vinci are famous all over the world, as is the Japanese artist Katsushika Hokusai. Almost everybody has seen or heard of da Vinci's The Last Supper or Hokusai's The Great Wave off Kanagawa. These images can be seen in books, or on the Internet; they are used in advertisements, or sold as merchandise like T-shirts, cups, file folders, magnets, or clocks. Even hundreds of years after they were created, the images are everywhere, and there is a good reason for this. They inspire awe and wonder and tickle the imagination.

Activity: Your knowledge of art

A)   *Name three artists whose work you have seen, or who you have heard of.*
B)   *What kind of artwork did they do?*
C)   *What is the artwork's name or content?*
D)   *Where was this artist from and when was this artist alive? (Of course, you probably don't know exactly places or years, but try to guess the general area and time when this person was alive.)*
E)   *What are some examples of merchandise that use images of fine art? (One example is an image of Van Gogh's Sunflowers on dishes and cups.)*

Criteria to be Art

From the 1300s (the beginning of the Renaissance), until the late 1800s, it was easy to define fine art. High-ranking members of society like popes, kings, the aristocracy, and rich merchants decided what was art. People with money and power commissioned talented artists to create works for public places like churches and squares, as well as for private spaces like personal libraries and dining rooms.

Moreover, there were entire institutions (similar to very powerful national universities) that determined if a painting or sculpture was worthy to be called art. There were, for instance, the Royal Academy of Arts in Britain, and the Academy of Beaux-Arts in France. Artists submitted their works to exhibitions held by these institutions. The exhibitions were called salons. If the salon accepted their work, then it was considered "fine art" and put on display. If the salon rejected their work, then it was not considered "fine art" and largely forgotten.

During this time, we may say there were some criteria for deciding what was art:

1. **Artist's intention**. The artist's goal was, quite simply, to create a work of fine art.
2. **Skill**. The artist had great talent and skill. If she or he was a painter, for instance, this meant having great painting skills. She or he was at least better than the average person, and the ones with the greatest skill were considered masters.
3. **Originality**. The artwork was original in that it was "one-of-a-kind". Though the artwork may resemble another work of art (there were, for example, countless paintings of the Madonna, mother of Jesus Christ), the actual work had a particular detail, style, composition, perspective, palette (colors), or some other content that had never been done before. Though someone who was good at copying other works would be considered talented, one had to produce something *original* to be a true artist.
4. **Spectators.** Spectators simply means people who look at an artwork. However, during these five hundred years, spectators meant those who were part of the "art world". In this case, "art world" means viewers who are knowledgeable about art. For an art work to be considered real art, somebody in the art world had to think it was art. If nobody thought it was art, then it wasn't art. In the 14th to late 19th century in Europe, the "art world" meant experts connected to art institutions, as well as art collectors, and art critics. Art critics are people who write their opinions of artworks in books, newspapers, journals, and magazines.

Activity: Art criteria

A) Which of the four criteria do you think are valid? All of them? Some of them? None of them? Explain.
B) Which of the four criteria do you think are most important and must never be broken? Explain.

Activity: Applying the criteria

● *Look at the chart below and decide whether the following things are art or not. Explain your reason using the four criteria above, or your own personal criteria.*

	Art or Not Art?	Reason
1. Mount Fuji		
2. A painting of Mount Fuji		
3. A photograph of Mount Fuji		

4. A tea bowl for a Japanese tea ceremony		
5. A Hello Kitty mug		
6. A paper cup		
7. Swimming		
8. Synchronized swimming		
9. Flowers in a garden		
10. Flowers arranged in the *ikebana* style		
11. A can of soup		
12. A painting of a can of soup		

Revised Criteria to be Art

The four criteria listed above are not quite the same today. Something very important happened in France in 1863. Artists whose works were rejected by the French Salon—including the famous artist Edouard Manet—decided to hold their own salon (called the "exhibition of rejects") as a protest and a way to show their art to the public. A few years later, Impressionist artists like Claude Monet also participated in this independent salon to protest the traditional and old-fashioned art tastes of the national French Salon. This act of rebellion among artists changed the history of art forever. It was the beginning of what is called Modern Art.

Even so, acceptance by the art world was still necessary. Now, however, the "art world" included members of society who were not only associated with official salons. This period gave greater freedom to the artist and made way for many new styles of art.

Despite the influence of this movement, for something to be considered a work of art, it still had to fulfil the above four criteria. It wasn't until 1917 that these four criteria would be greatly challenged.

Ready-made art

Although Pablo Picasso is probably the most famous artist of the 20th century, there is another artist who today is considered the most influential artist of the last century. He was a French artist named Marcel Duchamp. In a survey conducted in Britain in 2004, professional artists and critics were asked to rank the 100 most important artworks of the 20th Century. The number one art piece, according to this survey, was an artwork "made" by Marcel Duchamp in 1917 called *The Fountain*. This artwork was, in fact, a urinal (a toilet for men) he

Figure 8 Fountain

bought in a supply store. All he did was sign his name on it (he actually used a fake name: R. Mutt), place it on a pedestal, and say, "This is art." The art world was shocked. It was a revolution in art.

Some may say this artwork only kept the first and most important rule from the criteria above: artist's intention. The artist said it is art, and therefore, it is art. Because it was an object he bought in a store, no skill was involved, so clearly the second criteria was missing. By the way, Duchamp called this kind of art item a "readymade". In other words, it was "already made" by someone else. All he did was change its classification from being just a *functional* item to being an *artistic* item.

However, there is a lot of debate about the third criteria. Since he was using an object created by another person, it could be argued that the third criterion of originality was also broken. On the other hand, it could be argued that, in fact, he was very original because he had the unique vision of using a common product like a toilet as a work of art. The object itself was not original but the *idea* connected to the object was totally original. It was his intention to shock the art world and to make the art world question what art is. Ever since Duchamp made this artwork, the *idea* of an artwork has been given as much value as the artwork itself. In fact, there is a whole movement of art called Conceptual Art, which is still popular in the 21st century. It's not about the skill, or even the artwork itself, but the idea of the artwork that is most important.

Finally, in considering Duchamp's *The Fountain,* we must consider the fourth criterion of acceptance by the art world, or more broadly, acceptance by an audience.

It seems that this criterion is still important even with Duchamp's work. But for Duchamp, the art world was not the rich patrons or even the professional art critics. For Duchamp, the art world meant anybody. This was also a revolution. This means your opinion is just as important as a gallery owner or museum curator. Art is for everybody. Art can be made by anyone and is for everyone. Indeed, if you re-read the first part of this chapter, you can see how important Marcel Duchamp was in the history of art. In today's world, our idea of art has been most influenced by his sculpture from 1917, which was nothing more than a toilet.

Activity: Readymade art

A) Which of the four criteria do you think Duchamp's The Fountain keeps, and which ones do you think it lacks? Explain.
B) Marcel Duchamp called the toilet he bought a readymade. Readymade means a common object that is turned into an artwork simply by intention. Do you think "readymades" can be art? In what ways are they art? In what way are they not art?
C) The contemporary artist Jeff Koons used readymades such as basketballs and vacuum cleaners for some of his "sculptures". What other objects would be good readymades? Please try to think of some interesting objects to use as readymades. Why are these objects interesting readymades? What do they signify?
D) Look at the Art or Not Art? section again. Consider again the chart of 12 things. Which ones would you re-categorize as art or not art based on the new conception of art after Duchamp?
E) After considering the revolution of Duchamp, do you think anything can be art? What is art, and what is not art?

In the 1960s, the Pop Art movement became popular worldwide. American artist Andy Warhol, one of Pop Art's most famous artists, followed Marcel Duchamp's example and used a kind of readymade for his artworks. In Warhol's case, the "readymades" were photographs. For example, he used a publicity photograph of the actress Marilyn Monroe and transferred it onto a canvas. He then painted parts of the image and the background different colors such as gold,

Figure 9 Marilyn Monroe by Andy Warhol.

blue and red. In this way, he was in fact fulfilling the four criteria of art, though his original source material was not his own (somebody else took the photograph).

Activity: Duchamp and Warhol

● *The difference between Duchamp's work and Warhol's work is that Warhol did a significant amount of artistic work on his painting. Although he did not take the original photograph, he made a lot of artistic decisions. Duchamp just signed his name on a pre-made toilet. Is there a difference? Are both of these art? Are neither of these art? Explain.*

As a final example, in 1998, the British artist Tracy Emin made a "sculpture" called *My Bed*. The sculpture was a real bed, with sheets and pillows on it, and with lots of other things scattered around it. It looked messy and chaotic. It was not her bed, but a simulation of how her bed looks. She called it art. It was symbolic of the chaotic and rushed life of someone in the modern world. Some people thought it was disgraceful and insulting to call it art. However, despite the negative reaction, many people thought it was a great work of art, and in 2014, *My Bed* was sold at a famous auction for over 2.5 million British pounds.

Activity: Life as art

A) Is a messy bed art?
B) Is Tracey Emin's simulation of a messy bed art? Which criteria does it fulfil? Which criteria does it lack? Explain.
C) Does the fact that *My Bed* was sold for so much money make a difference in deciding if it is art or not? Can something be art if it nobody wants to buy it? If somebody pays a lot of money for something, does that automatically make it art? Explain.

Subjective Aspects of Art

When we look at an art object like a painting, we have an immediate opinion about it. We may like it, or we may not like it. We may think it's beautiful or we may think it's ugly. We may think it is interesting, or we may think it is boring. These opinions are our personal tastes, what we call our *subjective* opinions.

Subjective opinions are based on many factors. They may be based on your cultural background, race, religion, gender, economic status, or age, to name just a few factors. A man, for instance, may find a painting of a nude woman to be beautiful. A woman may find this same painting to be sexist or exploitative of women. A religious person may find the painting to be indecent. Art's meaning depends on who the viewer is.

It should also be noted that *when* an artwork is produced will also affect how it is perceived. A painting of a nude woman by master figure artist Amedeo

Modigliani (1884-1920) was sold in 2015 for about $170 million. It is ironic because when the artist died in 1920, he had no money. Nobody wanted to buy his paintings. When he made his paintings in the early 20th century, they were too shocking to be popular. They showed nude women in "scandalous" positions. Today, many people who see these paintings don't think they are shocking or scandalous. They actually look mild compared to images often seen in media or on the Internet. So, clearly, our idea of beauty and decency changes with time.

Another factor that greatly influences the quality and perception of art is culture. In the 19th Century in Europe, there was a trend called *Japonisme*. Japonisme is a term used for the "Japanese style" or "Japanese aesthetic" of art. For example, Japanese *ukiyo-e* woodblock prints were very popular among artists in the late 19th Century. Vincent Van Gogh was a big fan of Japanese art and had a collection of about 400 Japanese woodblock prints. In fact, Japanese art influenced the style of many European and American artists from the late 19th Century to today. If this is so, then it must be true that there is an aesthetic sense particular to Japanese art. Japanese art looked so different to European artists of that time. One of the features of Japanese art that was, and still is, so attractive to Westerners is its minimalism of color and line. Minimalism means using as few lines and colors as possible to convey a particular sense or scene. It doesn't mean simple, however. Actually, minimal art is very advanced and difficult to do.

Activity: Artistic differences

A) What are some cultural factors that may influence your impression of a work of art?
B) Do you think Japanese and Western people have different general tastes in art, or does it vary from person to person?
C) What are some features of older Japanese art as in woodblock prints?
D) What are some features of newer Japanese art as in anime and manga?
E) How do you think your gender, age, economic status may influence your impression of a work of art?
F) Think of a work of art—a movie, a comic book, a sculpture, a song—and consider how this work of art may be perceived differently depending on the person. What, specifically, may someone like or not like about a particular work of art?

Objective Aspects of Art

Art clearly has many subjective factors, and some people may believe that art can only be judged subjectively. However, there is also a strong argument to be made that art can be judged objectively. At the least, we can say that there are some objective features of art that can be judged. The two broadest features are: (a) naturalistic art and (b) abstract art.

Naturalistic art means the image in the painting (art work) looks somewhat similar to an image in real life. An apple in the painting looks somewhat like a real apple. A tree looks like a tree. The *Mona Lisa*, painted in the early 16th century, for instance, is a naturalistic portrait. It looks like a woman sitting in front of a landscape. It is easy to understand what you are seeing.

Abstract art means the image in the painting (art work) doesn't look much like an image in real life. Or it doesn't look at all like such an image. In 1911, Pablo Picasso painted an image of a person playing the accordion (*The Accordionist*, 1911), but it's very hard to see the person's head, body, and instrument. This is because it was painted in a kind of abstract style called Cubism. The objects are meant to represent real-life things but they don't look much like real-life things. Or, at least, it is hard to see the resemblance.

Then there is even purer abstract art, which doesn't look like any real-life thing, and isn't supposed to look like any real-life thing. It's purely an image made in the artist's mind. It may be an image that represents an emotion or idea. A good example of this is Mark Rothko's painting *Untitled (Red, Orange)*, from 1968. It's a large canvas with a few different colored large rectangles on it, and that is all. It doesn't represent anything from the real world. It is simply meant to represent human emotions.

So, if you want to consider art objectively, you can begin by considering whether the work is naturalistic or abstract. After that, there are other features you can consider to judge the work objectively. There are actually quite a few, but for our study let's consider three of the main ones: (1) color, (2) line, and (3) composition.

Colors can be placed into two main groups: warm colors and cool colors. Yellow is a classic warm color, and blue is a classic cool color. A painting whose colors are mostly warm will tend to be perceived as a cheerful painting, and a painting whose colors are mostly cool will tend to be perceived as a sad painting. Of course, these are generalizations, but they are often true.

Line means the different lines used in the artwork. These lines can make clear shapes like circles and squares, or they can be unclear and make no recognizable shape. The lines can be horizontal, vertical, or diagonal. Lines can give a sense of movement or stillness. They can look like they are coming together or moving apart from each other. When you look at a work of art, notice the lines. What are the lines doing? Are they thick or thin? Are they neat or messy? All of these things will help you understand the work of art and judge it.

Painting, and photography as well, are dependent on composition. Composition means the way the images are arranged in the picture. All pictures have a boundary. This is called the frame. Some pictures have a rectangular frame. Some have a square frame. How the content is arranged and the relationship between the content and the boundary, this is called composition. What is in the center of the frame? What is near the edges of the frame? How are all these elements connected within the frame? Asking yourself these questions will help you to judge a picture. Furthermore, a composition is not only what is inside the picture, but also what is not included in the picture. For example, a painting may show a man looking at something with a scared look on his face. But we can't see what he is looking at because it is outside the boundary of the picture. It is a mystery, and it makes us wonder what is going on. Thus, composition includes both what we see and what we can't see.

Activity: Analysing art: objective and subjective criteria

● *Some famous paintings will be shown in class. To warm up, for each painting, give a subjective opinion. Do you like this painting or not? Why?*

A) *Now, for the harder part. For each painting, give a detailed, objective analysis. For your analysis, you should consider the main components: naturalistic art, abstract art, color, line, and composition. Remember for this kind of analysis, you should avoid saying, "I like it" or "I don't like it". Rather, you should analyze this work of art by considering the elements of color, line, and composition.*

B) *Suggestions for paintings to be shown (images of all paintings are available online):*

C) *Vincent Van Gogh: Sunflowers, 1888*

D) *Edvard Munch: The Scream, 1893*

E) *Leonardo DaVinci: Salvator Mundi, 1490*

F) *Mark Rothko: Untitled (Black on Grey), 1970*

G) *Grant Wood: American Gothic, 1930*

H) *Georges Braque: Glass on a Table, 1909-10*

I) *David Bomberg: The Mud Bath, 1914*

J) *Wassily Kandinsky, Composition IV, 1913*

As a final note in this section, it is safe to say that one can enjoy a day at a museum without ever studying anything about art. Millions of people do that every day. Art can be enjoyed by people of all ages, whether or not they have any particular training in how to understand art. However, it is also true that if you have an education in art, your experience of art will be much richer and deeper. Also, the more you know about a particular painting, the more you can enjoy it. The points discussed in this section should help you look at art more objectively and be able to have a deeper, more meaningful experience when you look at art. To fully appreciate art, both your subjective and objective opinions should be considered.

Part 2. The functions of art

Art and Self-development

Art—paintings, photographs, music, movies, and more—can make us feel and think more deeply about the world, others, and ourselves. Think about a time when you watched a movie and started crying. Maybe there was a character in the movie you felt sorry for, and you were crying for that character. In this way, the movie made you feel empathy for another person. Empathy is part of our human nature, but sometimes we become too concerned about ourselves and forget to consider our feelings of empathy or sympathy. Art has the power to jolt us out of our selfishness and forces us to look at things with fresh eyes. As such, art can help us increase our level of caring for others. It also reminds us of the difference between right and wrong and may even give us a new idea of what it means to be a good person.

What is more, artworks can show us a perspective we never knew existed. Through art, we learn to see the world from the perspective of people from different times and cultures. We see people working hard, resting, suffering, laughing, celebrating. In short, we see others doing all the things that we ourselves do. In this way, artworks remind us of our core values as people, what it means to be human. It can remind us to show more gratitude to our parents or inspire us to do something nice for strangers. Characters in movies may show us how to act more heroically, how to be more open minded, how to behave with good manners. We are reminded of our moral duty to help others: family members, neighbours, people who are poor or who have experienced great loss. Thus, if we are open to the messages contained in art, we can develop as people.

Activity: Art and self-development

A) *Think of a movie that had a great impact on you. What did the movie make you think or feel? Was it related to morality, emotions, society, or something else? Explain.*
B) *Think of a song that moves you. What feature of the song moves you (melody, words, tempo)? What does the song make you think or feel?*
C) *Name another work of art—a photograph, painting, illustration, sculpture—and explain how this work of art helped you realized something deeper about yourself and/or the world.*

Art and Politics

Art and politics can be very closely related. Throughout history, governments and political movements have used art to help gain support. When art is used for political purposes, if the intention is sincere and honest, it is considered "promotional material". However, if it turns out art is being used to mislead or control people, we call it "propaganda". Sometimes the difference between promotional material and propaganda is not clear, or it is a matter of interpretation. Let's looks at some cases.

(1) After the French Revolution in 1789, when Napoleon Bonaparte became the head of the government in France, painters worked to depict him as a courageous, romantic and strong leader. One of the most famous paintings in history, done by Jacques-Louis David, shows Napoleon in uniform, riding a beautiful white horse while crossing the Alps (*Napoleon Crossing the Alps*, 1801). Eventually, Napoleon was exposed as a ruthless leader and was forced to resign his position and go into exile. The painting, which at first was thought of as promotional artwork for the new government, was later considered to be a kind of propaganda for a man who tried to take over much of Europe.

(2) In the Russian Revolution of 1917, the Russian monarch was overthrown by revolutionaries. This led to the establishment of a communist government and a new state called the Soviet Union. Around this time, Russian painter Kazimir Malevich made a painting of a black square. The entire painting was just one large black square. His paintings were an abstract form of art that was very different from any art that had been produced before. The simplicity of the image and its great departure from previous painting styles was a symbol that the old system had changed and that a new one was now beginning. Just as the Russian people had revolted against their historically repressive government, his painting was a revolt against the history of painting. The fact that his art was abstract is important. Naturalistic art was for the past. Abstract art represented the future, a future where everyone was equal. This concept was related to the new communist system of the nation.

(3) During the Great Depression in the 1930s, U.S. President Franklin D. Roosevelt created the Works Progress Administration (WPA). This government project hired architects, painters, and sculptors to create new buildings across the U.S. In this case, President Roosevelt's objective was to restore the American people's faith in their government and the economy. This art project wasn't to support a revolution but, rather, to help people restore their faith in the existing system. It was to give them a sense of hope that the hard times were ending and that the country was recovering. Grand-sized buildings with sculptures and paintings of hard working laborers

conveyed the message of a strong nation. It helped Americans believe that the U.S. was still rich and powerful nation with a better and brighter future ahead of it.

Activity: Propaganda and art

A) *Which of the above cases seem like promotional material? Which seem like propaganda? 2. Think of some examples of how art imagery was used by your, or another, country's government in the past to convey a particular image of power, strength, or happiness.*
B) *Think of some images still being used today by governments to send certain messages. What is the image? And what is the message?*
C) *The image of the comic book character Superman standing in front of the American flag is a powerful image of strength and nationalism. Since it is a comic book, we call it commercial art (rather than government-sponsored art, or fine art), but it is still a kind of propaganda. Think of at least one commercial image that conveys a certain idea of your culture (or another culture). Describe the image and the message.*

Art as a human universal

In the 1990s, two Russian migrants living in the United States, Vitaly Komar and Alexander Melamid, conducted an unusual study.[53] They did a series of surveys, using consumer research companies as well as online questionnaires, to gain information about people's preferences regarding art in eleven different countries. Their idea was to mimic the democratic political process in art, by getting people to identify what they most liked. Then, they created a series of paintings that matched the preferences of people in each country.

Activity: Komar and Melamid Survey

Some of the survey questions that they asked	
Paintings: higher goal or nice to look at?	
Prefer realistic or different looking?	
Prefer representation of reality or imagination?	
Prefer bold and stark or playful and whimsical?	
Prefer sharp angles or soft curves?	

---

[53] JoAnn Wypijewski, *Painting by numbers: Komar and Melamid's scientific guide to art*, Farrar Strauss Giroux, 1997.

Prefer geometric or random uneven patterns?	
Prefer expressive brush-strokes or smooth canvas?	
Prefer blended or separate colors?	
Prefer vibrant, paler or darker shades?	
Prefer more serious or more festive?	
Prefer busy or simple?	
Prefer famous or ordinary people?	
Prefer one person or group of people?	

You can see examples of the results of the questionnaires, expressed in their artwork, at the following link: <http://awp.diaart.org/km/painting.html>. Overall, abstract art, jagged shapes, colors like gold, orange, and yellow, were unpopular. In contrast, scenes with water, people, and animals were liked by many people.

Denis Dutton suggests that the paintings they made to represent people's favourite art are just jokes. By asking people what they liked and putting as many of the things that were popular as possible together, you don't necessarily get a picture that will be popular. Dutton uses the analogy of food: if you ask lots of people their favourite foods, you might discover, to little surprise, that people like ice-cream, pizza, hamburgers, fried chicken, and chocolate. But if you put them all together in one dish, people probably will not rush to buy it...

All the same, many scholars found it significant that people in Kenya, Iceland, China, and the United States all reported similar preferences about the kind of landscapes they liked: open areas with a few trees, water, people, and animals were universally popular. Some argued that the globalization of Western art, and especially landscapes, is the cause of this preference. But since even small children say they like this kind of composition, it seems quite possible that this preference is innate to humans. The fact that this idealized pattern fits the African landscapes in which human beings originally evolved may be rather significant.

Figure 10 Paintings reflecting Melamid and Komar's Survey Results

Especially, we seem to enjoy looking at habitats that are good for us to live in: grasslands with trees and water, with animals and fruiting and flowering plants.

These kinds of tendencies seem to have a direct relationship with the production of visual art: we enjoy the representations of ideal landscapes, food, living things, and people, in rich colors and textures and materials and so on. The same may go for music, with rhythms and tones in music matching the way that our brains organize the sounds of the natural world. Displays of physical fitness and muscularity in dance, as well as in nudes, similarly may be thought to be connected to evolutionary preferences, as youthfulness and strength suggest higher reproductive potential.[54] The origins of art, and the popularity of certain kinds of art, is recently considered to be a factor of human nature, and the way that humans have evolved (see Appendix A).

Conclusion

Art is everywhere, and it impacts us in the deepest of ways. Since it is everywhere, we tend not to notice it all the time, and tend not to give it enough attention. Much of our lives are structured by the art and design we use and see every day. By paying closer attention to art, by considering the subjective and objective features of art, and by understanding how art is often used to influence our thinking, we can live a fuller and richer life.

Appendix. Art as a human universal

1. Expertise: art involves special technical skills, which are recognized and admired.
   Becoming a great musician requires many thousands of hours of training and lessons; audiences enjoy, recognize and admire the musical arts that are the product of such technical development. The same goes for writers, sculptors, dancers, singers, and so on.

2. Non-utilitarian pleasure: people enjoy art for what it is, not because it is useful.
   People generally don't watch *Romeo and Juliet,* listen to hip-hop, or sing in choirs because they think it will help them get a job or make more money, but because they enjoy those experiences for what they are.

3. Style: art objects and performances follow rules that define different styles, forms, genres.
   Christian church music has a general pattern, and there are variations within that pattern for different hymns, carols, and so on. At the same time, newness and originality, which are the result of going against or ignoring convention and rules, including by combining different styles or rules, are sometimes praised.

4. Criticism: people judge and appreciate and interpret artworks.
   Newspaper and TV critics, academics, politicians, ordinary people all like to discuss and praise and criticize artworks that they experience, from drama shows to games and movies and theatre, in ways that they do not for, say, the fastest horse or the highest jumper.

---

[54] Pinker, *The blank slate*, *op. cit.*

5. Imitation: artworks usually imitates or represents real aspects of the world.

        Most art represents, in stylized ways, some aspect or aspects of the real world; especially paintings, sculpture, dance, and so on, and we can enjoy these representations for their realism, their skill, or for what the object itself is.

6. Special focus: art is separated from everyday life and made dramatic.

        Concerts and plays are performed on stages in special venues, paintings and photographs given elaborate frames, statues put on bases, performers wear special clothes, and so on.

7. Imagination: artists and audiences imagine possible other worlds in their minds, and their imaginations in particular.

        Animation, manga, science fiction, along with painting and classical literature and so on, all have as their theme *hypothetical worlds*, or what could exist—it's a "make-believe" world, even if it is based on or refers to the real world.

Denis Dutton, *The art instinct: beauty, pleasure, and human evolution*, Bloomsbury Press, 2009.

Chapter 7 Faith and religion

Russell Garofalo

Part 1. The meaning of faith

Faith and Religion are two closely related topics that are often discussed separately. However, in this chapter, we will discuss them together. The reason is because religion in fact depends on faith, so we must have an idea of what faith is before we can study the subject of religion deeply.

Faith is such a fundamental part of the human psyche that we use it in both religious and secular or non-religious ways. It is a hard word to define because of this reason. For example, in English we have various expressions that use the word "faith".

A) I have faith in God.
B) I have faith in you.
C) I have faith that the Hanshin Tigers will win the championship.
D) I have faith.

Activity: The meaning of faith

● *What do you think the above expressions mean? You may not be sure, but for each one, please guess the meaning.*

Now, that you have guessed, let's look at the meanings. The first expression (a) is clearly related to religion. To have faith in God means to believe in God; that is, to believe God exists. It may also have a secondary meaning that not only do you believe God exists, but also you believe that God is good and will take care of you.

The second expression (b), while its roots may come from religion, is used in a secular sense. To have faith in someone means that you trust someone, trust their ability, that they will do what is right, that they will succeed, and so on. It's a positive expression that you say to a friend, a family member, or somebody you respect.

As for the third expression (c), to have faith in a sports team's ability to win just means that you want them to win. There may be good reasons why you think they will win, or there may be no reason at all. Either way, fans of a team can be heard saying this. It is more about a desire than an actual logical reason or act of faith.

Finally (d), to have faith, when this is said in a general sense, it just means you have a positive attitude about the outcome of an event or situation. You want the outcome to be good, and you are keeping a positive attitude that the outcome will be good. This sentence can also mean "I am a religious person."

Thus, when we use the word "faith", sometimes we are talking about faith in the strict sense, and sometimes it is just a word that means "strong desire" or "positive attitude".

Conversely, we also have the expressions like the following: (a) "I lost faith in him"; (b) "I don't have faith in the New York Yankees"; (c) "I lost my faith." In order, these refer to: (a) losing the trust you have in someone; (b) not believing your team is good enough to win; (c) no longer believing in any religion. In these cases, it is not about desire. It is, in some sense, a more sober, more reflective assertion. Having faith means being happy and feeling hopeful. Not having faith means being negative and feeling hopeless about something. Although not having faith may be a more honest feeling, it is also a lot more painful. This is perhaps why most people choose to have some faith in something, whether it be God, science, pop stars, or sports teams. Life looks a lot brighter if you have hope.

We are starting to get a clearer idea of what faith is, and what it isn't. Let's consider our investigation of faith more deeply by comparing it with the closely related word *belief.* Again, it would be helpful to look at some common English expressions to understand the difference.

A)   I have faith in you.
B)   I believe in you.
C)   I believe you.
D)   I believe in God.

Activity: Faith and belief

● *What do you think are the differences between these four sentences? Do you think some sentences have the same meaning? Try to guess their meanings.*

Sentences (e) and (f), in fact, mean the same thing. To believe in someone is the same as having faith in someone, which we have already considered. However, sentence (g) is different. To believe someone means that you think what that person is saying is the truth. To say you *believe in someone* is very different to saying you *believe someone. To believe in someone* is to have a positive feeling about that person's ability or chances of success. *To believe someone* is simply saying you think the person is telling the truth, and not a falsehood. Sentence (h), to believe in God, has the same meaning as to have faith in God. It means you think God exists.

There are some nuances in the uses of the words *faith* vs. *belief*. We would say, "I believe in ghosts", but we wouldn't say, "I have faith in ghosts." We use "believe in" to mean belief in the existence of both religious and non-religious things (for example, God, ghosts, and aliens).

Activity: Religious and secular faiths

A) *Who or what do you believe in?*
B) *Who or what do you have faith in?*
C) *What are some examples of secular faith? Example: "My friend would never say anything bad about me behind my back."*
D) *What are some examples of religious faith? Example: "God created the world in seven days."*

Faith as part of human nature

Faith seems to be a unique feature of human beings, and a necessary feature that all human beings have. We could not function if we did not have faith. In its simplest sense, faith is a thought about something that we can't see, or something that hasn't happened yet. Faith is a part of our daily life. For instance, you have faith every time you sit in a classroom. You have faith in the fact that when the bell rings at the end of class, the class will be over. Your teacher will not keep teaching you for another hour. At least, you hope not! In its basic sense, this is what we mean by faith. Faith is using your past experience to help you predict the future. It is also using logic and experience to understand the present. When I close the refrigerator door, I have faith that the light goes out. This belief comes from what I know about machines and how they work.

Activity: Faith in context

A) *Make a list of five (or more) situations that require "faith".*
B) *Now look at these situations more closely. Do they refer to future, present, or even past events? Explain.*
C) *Are all these situations about faith, or are some actually about wishes or desires? Explain.*

Perhaps it is becoming clear now that faith is involved in almost, if not all the events of our lives. Faith is a constant. For example, I make an appointment to meet my friend, and I have faith that my friend will come to that appointment. If faith is part of everything we do or think, you might wonder, is this topic really about faith? Isn't this topic actually about reason and our logical reasoning ability? If you are wondering this, you are right. They are, in fact, very closely related. Let's look at an example.

Here is a logical sequence of thoughts:

a. Every time I have used my favorite mechanical pencil in the past, it has made a nice, clear mark on the page.
b. I am using my favorite mechanical pencil now.
c. My mechanical pencil is going to make a nice, clear mark on the page.

In this example, you are clearly using your logical ability to predict the future. However, it is not certain that your mechanical pencil will work right now. Faith is a "little something extra", a positive belief about something. It is a mixture of desire and logic. It is also trust in yourself and your power to control the future. If you believe something, it will become true. At least, you hope so. This is a key part of faith: the idea that if you profess it to be so, it *will* be so. It is a kind of affirmation, sometimes fully supported by evidence, like scientific evidence, and sometimes not supported by any evidence.

What is interesting about faith is that you do not need to be religious to have faith, as we have seen. Many people who have no religion still believe in spiritual or supernatural things. For instance, someone may say they don't believe in God, but they do believe in ghosts. Or, they may not believe in God but they do believe certain superstitions. One famous superstition is that if you break a mirror, you will have seven years of bad luck. It seems many people believe this, even those who do not have any religion and don't believe in supernatural phenomena.

Activity: Superstitions

A) *Make a list of five common superstitions.*
B) *Which of these superstitions do you believe? Which don't you believe?*
C) *Why do you believe some but not others?*
D) *What is the basis of your belief, or disbelief, in these superstitions? (For example, your mother told you; you think it's logically possible; everyone you know believes this)*

Faith and Religion: what's different?

As we have seen, faith is part of everyday life. If you are a non-religious person, but a believer of science, you would say that faith is built into our brains. That is, you believe faith is a basic structure of our psychology. Religion is just an outcome of this basic feature of faith. Thus, if you are a non-religious person, you might believe religion developed like this:

A) First, we are born with the psychological skill of "having faith" built into our brains. At birth, it is a secular skill as we discussed earlier.
B) We observe the world around us.
C) We make conclusions about the things we can't easily explain like fire, thunder, suffering, and death. We make up things like gods, God, miracles, demons, and the devil to explain difficult things.
D) Formal religions are formed.

On the other hand, if you are a religious person, you may think about religion like this:

A) God exists and creates all things.
B) Humans are made from God.
C) God gives us the ability to know God. This is called faith.
D) Religion develops from God's instructions.

The purpose of this chapter is, of course, not to persuade you to have one, some or no religion. The purpose is to investigate how deeply faith and religion are part of our psyche, our cultures, and our history until this point in time.

Simply put, faith includes thoughts that are secular or religious (or both) in nature.

Religion is a formal institution based on a particular set of faiths. In today's world, increasing numbers of people are growing up with no religion. Even for those who claim to have a religion, many times this is in name only. A person may identify herself as Christian or Buddhist simply because that is the religion of her grandparents and parents. She doesn't have any particular faith, but she has, by default, a religion.

In fact, it could be argued that many people who have claimed to have a religion are really only showing a kind of loyalty to their family. The reasoning goes like this: My mother is Catholic; I love and respect my mother; therefore, I follow the Catholic religion, too. This may seem a simple deduction, but it is also a powerful one that has affected the religious beliefs of millions, if not billions, of people in history.

Religion and the Right to Religious Privacy

The academic definition of "religion" is quite abstract. The French sociologist Emile Durkheim famously proposed that religion involves beliefs and practices that divide the world into the sacred and the profane (ideas about what is sacred / not-sacred, and ways that people act towards sacred and non-sacred things). Basically, Durkheim felt that there an ordinary everyday side to life, as well as a special side that we hold in awe and honor. Thus, for example, Catholicism involves a range of beliefs, for example, that Jesus Christ was the son of god, as well as practices related to this, such as the celebration of Christmas as a day commemorating Christ's birth. On the other hand, most people are not believed to be the child of god, and a birthday is special for just for the individual and their family and friends. These people and events are part of the profane world, while Christ and Christian practices and things are part of the profane or non-sacred world. The Christian religion, in short, divides the world into sacred and non-sacred areas. Because Durkheim's definition is so broad, it becomes possible to argue that people may have religious feelings towards nature, space, flags, atoms, or even idol groups!

For our purposes, however, we will follow a conventional definition of religion as a system of belief in a higher power like God, gods, or an Intelligent Creator. In today's world, an increasing number of people have no religion. This simply means they choose not to follow any formal religion. At the same time, billions of people in today's world have a religion, and their religion plays an important part in their values and lifestyle.

In many countries where the population consists of people with different religions, it has become proper etiquette *not* to ask another person's religion. In fact, it is considered an invasion of privacy to ask someone their religion. In some countries, it may even be illegal to ask someone's religion. The reasons are simple. People may be discriminated against because of their religion, or, on the other hand, they may receive special treatment because of their religion. Having no religion can also be a cause for discrimination. Thus, depending on the culture, if somebody asks about your religious beliefs, you could rightfully say, "That's a personal question. I'd rather not answer that." In other cultures, talking about one's religion or non-religion is no problem.

Activity: Religious privacy

A) *Is asking about someone's religion considered a personal question in your country? Explain your opinion.*
B) *As we read above, asking about someone's religion in some countries, for example the U.S., is a personal question. The reason is mainly because of the risk of discrimination or some bias based on the answer. (a) What specific kinds of discrimination do you think may happen to someone based on their religion? (b) Conversely, what kinds of preferential treatment might someone receive because of their religion?*
C) *In the U.S., there is a saying: "Never talk religion or politics at the dinner table". What does this mean? Why do you think these two topics are not good to talk about, rather than other things like sports, art, or movies? What is so controversial about these two topics that we shouldn't talk about them at the dinner table?*

Defining God

There are many different words for God, and many different ideas about who or what God is. So, if somebody asks you, "Do you believe in God?" a safe way to answer this question is to ask, "What do you mean by God?"

You might not believe in God as an old man with a beard who stands on clouds. And you might not believe in God as an Intelligent Force that created all the natural laws of the universe. However, if someone says, "God is Time", then maybe you could believe that. Or, if someone says, "God is Love", perhaps that is something you might believe, too. Maybe, though, you just don't like using the word God or talking about God at all. Of course, then it is always your right to say, "This is not a comfortable topic for me. Please let's talk about something else."

In today's world, though more and more people have no religion or religious beliefs, there are still billions of people who are religious. So, to better understand other people and cultures, it is helpful to know some basic facts about different religions.

Types of religious beliefs

All religious beliefs depend on the belief in a God, Force, Creator, First Mover, Intelligent Being, Soul, and/or Spirit. Religious beliefs can be classified into the following types:

1. **Monotheism**. This is the belief in a single God. One God created the world and everything in it.
2. **Polytheism**. This is the belief in many gods. There is a thunder god, a rain god, a sun god, a god of good harvests, a sea god, and so on.
3. **Pantheism**. This the belief that everything is God, and God is everything. God is everywhere, every time.
4. **Atheism**. This is the belief that there is no God. God does not exist. There is at least one major religion in the world that doesn't believe in any God but does believe in a kind of spirit or force that never dies.
5. **Agnosticism**. This is not normally a religion, although it could be. It is the belief that it is impossible to know whether God exists or not. Thus, these people don't believe in God, but they also don't deny the existence of God. They simply state that they don't know.

Activity: Detailing your religious knowledge

A) *Make a list of all the religions you can think of. You should be able to think of at least five religions pretty easily.*
B) *Look at your list. For each religion, decide if it is monotheistic, polytheistic, pantheistic, atheistic, or even perhaps agnostic.*
C) *Look at the list again. What are the basic beliefs of each religion? Who are the main "deities" or "holy people" associated with this religion?*
D) *Which religion has the most followers in today's world? Which has the second most followers? If you are not sure, guess. Hint: these two religions each have more than one billion followers (one billion = 1,000,000,000).*

Religion and daily life

Even if you are not a religious person, chances are your life is impacted by religious beliefs in some way. Your life is impacted probably in more ways than you think. For example, the yearly holiday calendar in many Western countries mostly revolves around major religious festivals. Some of these are the Christian festivals of Christmas and Easter, and the Jewish holiday of Yom Kippur. In many Asian countries, a major holiday is Buddha's birthday. Though you may not be religious, or even have any interest in religion, chances are you appreciate having these days off from school or work.

Activity: Religious holidays

1. Aside from the holidays already mentioned, what are some other religious holidays you know about? Try to think of at least two and explain them.

Perhaps even more powerful are the social customs that are connected to religion. Going to a shrine on New Year's Day is an example of a religious-based custom. Although New Year's Day is technically a non-religious holiday, in many countries there are religious connections to this day. As another example, many Christians "say grace" before eating a meal. This means people say a prayer to thank God for the food. In Japan, there is a similar custom of giving pause to say thanks before eating.

Even some words that have no particular religious significance today are actually words that originally came from a religious practice. For example, the word *breakfast* means "to break fast". In the past, after sunset it was forbidden to eat any food. Not eating food is called "fasting". So, every night people would fast. When the sun rose in the morning, people would be allowed to eat again. Thus, they would break their fast, and eat their morning meal. In time, this simply came to be known as breakfast.

Activity: Religious practices

A) *How is going to a shrine on New Year's Day connected to religion? What is the religious foundation for this custom?*
B) *Does* itadakimasu *have its foundation in religion? If you know, please explain. If you aren't sure, try to guess the meaning.*
C) *Make a list of some customs that you perform daily, monthly or yearly, and which are connected in some way to religion.*
D) *Look at your list from number 3 and try to explain the details of the custom and the religious belief connected to each custom.*

Religion and Science

Although it might seem that faith and science are opposite ways of thinking, in fact, the difference between them is not always so clear. In this section, we will list the different arguments about the relationship between God and science. If God does exist, what is the nature of this God? If God doesn't exist, how can we explain the existence of the universe and human beings? Some of these ideas overlap, and it will be interesting to discuss how they may be related.

(1) Some religious people called Creationists (people who believe in the literal meaning of the Bible) do not believe in evolution. They believe God created the Earth, Adam (the first man), and Eve (the first woman). According to them, the idea that humans evolved from apes is simply a belief that has no proof, like belief in ghosts or telepathy. They believe that those who believe in evolution are simply using their faith—faith in logic and faith in science—to conclude that humans came from apes.

(2) What is more, there are other non-religious people who also don't believe that humans naturally descended from apes. Some believe an alien race visited the earth and performed scientific experiments on animals, which resulted in the creation of human beings. Thus, when faith is involved, any belief is possible.

(3) At the same time, anything that requires faith can be doubted or questioned. *Logical positivists* are people who believe that only phenomena which can be proven through experimentation or that have clear evidence should be trusted. If you can't prove it exists, then you shouldn't believe it exists. They doubt the existence of God because they say God's existence can't be proven.

(4) Some argue that the simple fact the universe exists means God must exist. The universe must have a Creator (also called a First Cause or First Mover). Something (the universe) must have come from something (God). This, simply put, is part of the *cosmological argument*.

(5) Others believe that the universe is so perfectly balanced and harmonious that some Intelligent Creator, or God, must have made it. This is called the argument of *Intelligent Design*.

(6) Then, of course, there is Charles Darwin's theory of evolution. The theory of evolution says that the "fittest survive". That is, those who are best able to survive will pass their DNA to their offspring. With each generation, then, the number of positive traits will continue to increase. In other words, creatures like humans are getting more and more perfect every generation. Evolutionists are against the idea of

a God who created the perfect human from the beginning. The perfect human does not exist yet, but someday, according to evolution, it might. This theory seems to contradict the idea of *Intelligent Design*.

(7) However, the debate is not over yet. With all the new knowledge available from findings in physics, we see that the universe is made up of tiny particles smaller than the atom. These particles are all interconnected. Physicists have even found what they call the "God Particle" which they believe exists everywhere in the universe. If this is true, then *Intelligent Design* may be true after all. Although the creatures on earth are still evolving, the universe itself already has a perfect structure from the beginning.   (8) But wait. The debate is still not over. There are some who believe the universe has always existed. In fact, nobody created the universe. It always existed and will always exist.

(9) Some believe the Big Bang was the beginning of the universe, and that before the Big Bang there was nothing. Those who believe in the Big Bang could easily believe that there is no Intelligent Creator. The Big Bang just happened. The universe is "something" coming from "nothing". It is what is called the "uncaused first cause". That is, it the first event of the universe (first cause), but nothing made it happen (uncaused). It just happened.

(10) The Big Bang actually did not come from nothing. It came from a very small and very dense amount of mass that exploded to form the universe. So, one may still wonder where this small amount of mass came from, and why this mass suddenly exploded. If you think about that, you may decide that there must have been a First Mover (also known as God) that created the original mass and made it explode.

(11) Combinations of the above ideas, new ideas not yet discovered, or your own ideas are all possible, too. In fact, what people know is always changing, so new ideas should always be welcomed.

To conclude this section, if you are a logical thinker, in fact this debate never ends. You could keep finding reasons to support one or the other side about God's existence. And in the end, it may always come back to the question we have already considered: What do you mean by God?

Activity: Comparing faith types

A)   *Are religious faith and secular faith the same or different? In other words, is "faith" simply a part of the human mind, and religion just one form of faith? Or, is religious faith different? Explain.*

B) *What are five of the most common events or phenomena that some people believe exist, while other people don't believe? Make a list and discuss.*

C) *What do you think about the "Big Bang"? Who or what caused the Big Bang? What do you believe existed before the Big Bang?*

D) *Does Western science have the authority to say "the scientific way is the only way"? Some people may argue that requiring "empirical evidence" rather than "just belief" is a kind of cultural imperialism. What do you think?*

Part 2. The functions of religion

The benefit of believing in something

Humans seem to have a deep need to believe that their lives will not end with death. This may be the strongest reason for faith and religion. The thought that our lives end when we die is frightening.

For this reason, even non-religious people often say they believe in some kind of afterlife, or some kind of spirituality. Some people say, "I am not religious, but I am spiritual." Even people who say they are not religious or spiritual still have something they believe in. It is a deep part of the human psyche: the need to hold onto something, the need to have hope. The idea of becoming nothing is against our built-in ability to dream, imagine, and have hope for the future. It is against our will to survive.

Even non-religious atheists and agnostics take comfort in the idea that the universe has a self-contained amount of energy and matter. From a physics perspective, nobody can ever escape the universe. We always were and will always be part of the universe because the total amount of energy and matter in the universe is always the same.

A study published in October 2017 suggest that a person may know when he or she has died. That is because brain activity continues for a short amount of time after a person is clinically dead. Dr Sam Parnia, from the NYU Langone School of Medicine in New York City, suggests that since brain activity continues after a person's heart has stopped beating, the brain is still working and may still produce thoughts. These thoughts may include awareness that the person has just died. Even though the heart has stopped beating, and there is no more blood flowing through the body, the chemical reactions happening in the brain will take some time—how long is not clear—to stop happening. During that time, the brain will recognize that the body is dead, and the brain will communicate those thoughts in the final moments of consciousness. For non-religious people this seems like a truly frightening idea: to be told by yourself that you're dead, to know you're dead, to believe there is nothing coming next. However, for religious people who have a strong sense of faith in a higher power like God, or a belief in the continuance of the spirit like reincarnation, knowing you have died is perhaps not as scary. Your brain will recognize you are dead, and then your belief system will take over. If your brain is still working then your imagination must still be working. Those who believe and can imagine an afterlife will start to imagine that afterlife as a way of holding onto hope.

Blaise Pascal (1623-1662) proposed a bet that you could not lose. Basically, his idea was that believing in some kind of God was a "win-win" situation. If you believe in God, and God does exist, then you win. On the other hand, if you believe in God, and God doesn't exist, then you still win because you have provided yourself with the comfort of a belief in God. This is commonly referred to as "Pascal's Wager". The scientific findings by Dr. Parnia in New York seem to support Pascal's Wager. If your brain knows you are dead, and you believe in God, then your brain will make up a story of God comforting you in death, whether or not God actually exists. Either way, you will be comforted by your beliefs, so you may as well believe in the most positive scenario about what happens after death.

Activity: Conditions for belief

A) *If you are a person of faith, what might make you a non-believer?*
B) *If you are a non-believer, what might make you have faith?*
C) *Some research suggests that people who have religious faith are happier than people who have no faith. (a) Do you think this might be true? (b) Why might this be true?*
D) *Why might this not be true?*

Religion and Ethics

In many ways, people learn their sense of ethics from their religions. In the Old Testament of the Bible, for instance, the Ten Commandments outline the ten basic rules of ethical behaviour. "Thou shall not kill" is one of the most well-known of these ten rules. Another one is "Thou shall not covet thy neighbour's goods". This means, you shouldn't desire what other people have. In other words, appreciate what you have and do not make yourself suffer with jealousy. So, in this way, religious rules show people what they should or shouldn't do, not only for the well-being of others, but also for the health of their own mind and body. Ethical behaviour means behaviour that helps others as well as yourself.

Thus, religion has these rules that teach us about ethics. On another level, religion encourages us to behave nicely. The Christian concepts of Heaven and Hell help, in theory at least, people to behave nicely to each other. God is always watching (just like Santa Claus!). If you behave well, you will go to Heaven, which is like an eternal resort holiday. If you behave badly, you will go to Hell. And Hell is definitely not a pleasant place to spend all of eternity.

The Buddhist religion has a similar idea. If you behave well to others, and if you behave well to yourself by not letting yourself be tortured by too much desire, then you will be born again (reincarnate) into a higher being, or even reach Nirvana, the ultimate paradise. If you have too much desire, though, and cause pain for yourself and others, you will be born again into a lower being and continue to suffer.

So, religion teaches us ethical behaviour, but religion can also be the cause of unethical behaviour. Many people have killed for the sake of religion and have justified their killing as allowed by their religion for a certain cause. Or they have done something unethical like steal and rationalized their behaviour by saying, "God will forgive me. God forgives everything." In this way, people sometimes use religion as a license to do whatever they want. As long as they say "I'm sorry" and ask for God's forgiveness, everything will be all right in the end.

Thus, while it is true that religion can teach us ethical behaviours, we have to be careful not to let religious belief give us the freedom to do anything we want.

Activity: Religion and ethics

A) *What are some specific examples of ethical behavior promoted by religion? Explain.*
B) *What are some specific examples of people justifying unethical behavior with their religion?*
C) *Where did you learn your sense of ethics?*
D) *Do you think religion is mostly a good source of ethics?*
E) *What is the foundation of ethics? Is it human nature? Family? Society? What encourages you to behave politely and kindly?*

Religion and Politics

Throughout history, many people have been persecuted and killed in the name of religion. We can divide these religious persecutions into different categories.

(1) War. There have been numerous wars conducted over religion. The Thirty Years' War in the 17th Century was at least partly due to the conflict between the Protestant and Catholic religions.
(2) Government discrimination against those members of a particular religion. For example, a government may not allow members of a particular religion to wear certain types of religious clothing in public places.
(3) Government persecution (and sometimes genocide) of those members of a particular religion. In these cases, a government has persecuted those of a particular religion. Perhaps the most famous case in history is that of

Adolf Hitler and the Nazi Government of Germany in the 1930s and 1940s. They tortured and killed millions of men, women and children of the Jewish faith for no reason other than their religion.

(4) Government persecution of those with ideas that challenge the state religion. A famous example is Galileo Galilei (1564-1642) who was arrested for claiming that the earth revolved around the sun. This went against the religious belief that God created the Earth as the center of the world.

(5) Government persecution of anyone practicing any religion. During the years of the Soviet Union, all religions were banned. Christians and Jewish people in the U.S.S.R. had to worship in secret. In Poland, people could be arrested just for possessing books that contained even just single sentences about a belief in or the existence of God.

Activity: Religion and conflict

A) *Name and explain at least one armed-conflict (war) in history that was caused by religious differences.*
B) *Name and explain at least one instance of people being persecuted or discriminated against because of their religion.*
C) *What does "religious freedom" mean?*

The social functions of religion: community, understanding, meaning

Durkheim noted how religion is one of the key factors in the formation of human communities. Certain people decide what is sacred and what is not, *for them*. They choose places, things, peoples, beliefs, events, substances as sacred (or profane). Those sacred things then come to represent that community. As a result, the community is defined as the people who worship those sacred things. For example, certain people early in the 1st century A.D. decided that Christ was a sacred figure, and they began to worship him and his teachings. As they did so, Christianity became a core element that joined those people together: they formed a community of Christians. Further, by worshipping Christ, that community made itself sacred, and more important than the individual members who belong to it. This leads individuals to make sacrifices for the community itself. Some form of religion in this form is in fact necessary for communities to exist.

The German sociologist Max Weber, in his book, *The protestant ethic and the spirit of capitalism* (1905), argued that understanding religion is necessary to understand people. Simply put, he thought that religious beliefs affect people's view of reality, and therefore affect their actions in life. Basically, without knowledge of what people believe, it is impossible to understand why people do things. His work on the Protestant ethic and the development of capitalism is one of the most famous illustrations of this argument. Instead of saying that societies and economics shape religion, Weber tried to show that religions can shape societies and economies.

Focusing on Calvinist Protestants in Europe after the 16th century, Weber's noted how Calvinism taught that God had chosen some people to go to heaven even before those people were born (predestination). The problem, at least for believers in Calvinism, was that they didn't know who God had chosen. Faced with this uncertainty about whether they had been chosen by God, some people decided that being wealthy in this world must be a sign of God's approval. Influenced by this belief, many Calvinist Protestants tried to increase their wealth by hard work and smart investments. Basically, Calvinist Protestantism taught believers that good Christians should work hard, make money, and re-invest their money in business, and not spend their money on luxuries and pleasures. But as people acted in this way because of their religious beliefs, they actually ended up helping the development of capitalist economies, and industrialization! Over time, to update the story somewhat, the idea that successfully reinvesting and increasing one's capital would reveal that one had God's approval has weakened; now, people merely try and make money because they believe that is good, without worrying too much about what God thinks of them. At any rate, Weber's study shows that you can't understand the development of capitalism in Western Europe without knowing something about people's religious beliefs.

Finally, religion is also sociologically important because of its connection to human understanding of what life is about. The famous American sociologist Talcott Parsons once said that religion seems to be as universally human as language. All human societies ask questions about the meaning of life, whether there is anything after our lives end, and why our lives often involve needless suffering. Religions respond to these kinds of questions differently to science. Science can tell us *how* we live, and *how* we age and die. It explains these processes in a matter-of-fact way. But science doesn't say anything about *why* we live and age and die; it doesn't deal with the problem of *meaning*. In contrast, religions don't tell us about processes, but rather about significance. They tell us why we live, and what happens after we die, and explain why there is evil in the world, and so forth. In this way, religion works to reduce people's anxieties and worries, and so helps to stabilize society. Thus, for Parsons, religion was functionally very important.

Activity: Religion and community

A) *How can Durkheim's ideas about community and religion help us to understand contemporary nation-states?*
B) *How can Buddhism and Shintoism help us to understand people's actions in Japan?*

C) *Research what different religions teach about what happens when we die. Do your findings help support Parsons' thesis about the usefulness of religion?*

Modernity and religion

Many of the most influential sociologists believed that religions would weaken in the modern era, alongside industrialization and urbanization. The simple reason for their belief was that most religions were just a collection of myths that had little historical or scientific basis. As societies gained more scientific knowledge about the world, and improved their technological abilities to modify physical environments, religions would become obsolete, or unnecessary, although they might survive as personal hobbies. This way of thinking—that modern societies would become secular or non-religious—was known as the secularization thesis.

However, in recent decades, many critics have pointed out that it doesn't seem to be true. Looking at the world as a whole, a WIN/Gallup International poll from 2015 indicated that in over 25 countries, more than 95% of the population feels religious, with the rate high in Africa, the Middle East, South-East Asia, Latin America, and southern Europe especially. Only one country, China, had less than 10% of people feeling religious (7%), followed by Japan at 13%, and then Estonia at 16%, and Sweden at 19%. Most of Western Europe registered 30% or higher, as did the United States, where around 40% of the population attends a religious service every week. Modernization, wealth, and technological knowledge don't seem to cancel out religion automatically.

One reason for this may be related to Parsons' idea about the lack of meaning provided by modern science, with religion filling that gap. For many, religion is part of an individual search for meaning and identity. However, this search is clearly individual, with institutional religion being relatively less important.

Another reason may be that joining a religion provides people with a community to belong to and find comfort in. Jerome Kagan writes that Americans are much more involved in organized religion than Europeans because the United States has more economic competitiveness, more geographic mobility, more income range, less harmony, and less secure welfare nets. Religious communities help people to avoid social isolation and feel that their lives are meaningful.[55] The massive waves of urbanization, as well as domestic and international migration today, combined with increased job insecurity and mobility, growing income gaps, and less familiarity

---

[55] Kagan, *op. cit.*

with people in "our" neighbourhoods suggests that this kind of demand for religion may only grow.

A further idea is that as knowledge, beliefs, and values diversify and become relativized in the context of globalization, some people feel threatened by the apparent lack of certainty and turn to religion as a higher source of certain knowledge. Such people, whether Christian, Muslim, Shinto, Hindu or Buddhist, may become, quite literally, "fundamentalists".[56] However, a considerable proportion of people in contemporary societies do not believe in religion and take a more relativist view towards morals and values. These factors may help to explain the persistence of religious belief today, as well as the level of conflict related to religion.

Table 13 Social change and religious change

	Traditional society	Modern society
Economy / society	Agricultural / rural / settled	Industrial / urban / mobile
Worldview	Slow to change, past and community oriented,	Present and future-looking, progress and individual-oriented
Religious beliefs and practices	Collective / community truths that explain the world Linked to other social institutions	Less collective and more individual De-linked from other institutions Competing other truths

Conclusion: Religious tolerance and understanding

As our world becomes more globalized, it is reasonable to hope religious tolerance and understanding will be greater in the near future. Certainly, we should try to make this happen. Religious tolerance means accepting that people have different beliefs than you, and that all people have a right to believe what they want as long as this belief does not cause harm to others.

Religious tolerance and understanding spans the spectrum of not persecuting any people for their religion all the way to respecting someone when they can't do something, or must do something, because of their religion. For example, some days are holy days for people of a particular religion. A religious Christian should not be expected to work on Christmas, for instance. Or a religious Jewish person should not be expected to work on Yom Kippur, an important Jewish holiday. In addition, as religious Muslims pray five times a day, they need a place and time to pray even

---

[56] See, for example, Ulrich Beck, *A god of one's own*, Polity Press, 2010.

during work hours. Religious understanding means being sensitive to the different needs of religious people.

Though countries have not achieved true religious equality yet, some countries have made great progress toward reaching it. For the sake of domestic peace, international peace, and the advancement of human rights, seeking religious freedom and tolerance should be one of the primary goals of the global village. At the same time, we have to ensure that religion is not used as an excuse or justification for any kind of violence.

Activity: Religious intolerance

A) *Give at least one example of religious intolerance.*
B) *Give at least one example of religious tolerance.*
C) *Do you feel that there is religious tolerance in your country? Why or why not?*
D) *What can be done to show greater respect for people's religious beliefs?*

A

Abe Shinzo, 68
Adam Smith, 47
Akihito, 69
Alfred Nobel, 46
Andy Warhol, 130
Answer bias, 20
Art for art's sake, 124
Article 9, 72

B

Belief, 143
Biography, 62
Blaise Pascal, 153

C

Calvinism, 156
Causation, 42
Chiune Sugihara, 109
Common history, 71
Community of Christians, 155
Confirmation bias, 50, 84
Consistency, 100
Cyclical theories of history, 87

D

Deeper freedom, 55
Determinism, 52, 55
Deviance, 24
Dialectical emergence, 45
Dignity, 113
Duty, 112
Duty conflicts, 115

E

Economic Determinism, 89
Emile Durkheim, 146
Ethics, 96
Ethnocentrism, 107
Evidence, 64
Experiment, 8
Experiments in the human sciences, 33

F

Faith, 142
Fatalism, 58
Fernand Braudel, 87

Fine art, 125
Franklin D. Roosevelt, 136
Fundamentalists, 158

G

Genes, 44, 52
Geographical determinism, 87
Geohistory, 87
Globalization, 108, 158
God, 147
Graeme Allison, 88
Great Person Theories, 88
Group identity, 66

H

Helsinki Declaration, 36
Hindsight, 79
Hirohito, 69
History education, 69
Holism, 45
Human nature, 72
Human science, 16
Human universal, 137, 140
Hypothesis, 7

I

Immanuel Kant, 112
Individual filters, 75
Innovation, 89
Instinct, 97
Irony, 24
Irrationality, 26

J

Jacques-Louis David, 136
Japonisme, 132
Jeremy Bentham, 116
John Rawls, 113
John Stuart Mill, 121
Josef Stalin, 68

K

Karl Marx, 89
Kazimir Malevich, 136

L

Labelling theory, 24

Law of large numbers, 39
Linear theory of history, 88
Loaded questions, 22

M

Marcel Duchamp, 129
Marvin Minsky, 37
Max Weber, 48, 155
Money, 30
Moral reasoning, 99
Moral relativism, 104
Morality, 96

N

National flag and anthem, 22
National identity, 66
Nationalism, 84
Nuremberg Code, 36

O

Objective Aspects of Art, 132
Observation bias, 18
Okinawa, 73
Olympic Games, 27

P

Peers, 60
Philip Zimbardo, 35
Phillips Curve, 42
Primary Sources, 75
Probability, 38
Propaganda, 67, 77
Pseudo-science, 12

R

Racism, 76
Random variation, 38
Reactance, 26
Ready-made art, 129
Reductionism, 44
Religious persecution, 154
Richard Feynman, 7
Rule utilitarianism, 120

S

Samuel Bowles, 48
Scientific method, 8
Secondary Sources, 79
Self-aware, 18, 37, 46
Self-correcting, 37
Self-fulfilling prophecy, 23
Selfish, 108
Sex, 47
Significance, 63
Social Bias, 76
Social convention, 105
Special pleading, 100, 113
Stanford Prison Experiment, 35
Stanley Milgram, 33
Stereotype, 24
Steven Pinker, 88
Subjective Aspects of Art, 131
Superstition, 145
Surface freedom, 54
Symbolic interactionism, 47

T

Talcott Parsons, 156
Topic choice bias, 83
Tory history, 86
Tracy Emin, 131
Trends, 41
Truth, 102
Types of religious beliefs, 148

U

Unintended consequences, 47
Utilitarianism, 116

V

Value neutrality, 51
Veil of ignorance, 113
Vitaly Komar and Alexander Melamid, 137

W

Whig history, 86

Artwork credits

Fran Simo, I Dreamed About A Human Being, Flickr Cc By-Nc-Sa 2.0, P1. The Milgram Experiment, CC-By-SA-4.0 Wikipedia By Fred The Oyster; P. 33. The Libet Experiment Via Wikipedia Commons CC-BY-SA-3. P.57. Manipulated Photo Of Stalin, Via Wikipedia Commons, P.68. 1898 French Cartoon, National Library Of France / Henri Meyer, P. 77. Migita Toshihide, Surrender Of Chinese Forces After The Battle Of Weihaiwei, 1895, Wikipedia Commons, P. 78. The Trolley Problem, Wikipedia Commons. McGeddon CC BY-SA 4.0, p. 118. Fountain, In The Blind Man. Via Wikipedia Commons, P. 129. Marilyn Monroe By Andy Warhol, Pixabay Creative Commons, P. 130. Melamid and Komar, http://awp.diaart.org/km/index.html. P.138.

The authors

Russell Garofalo, Masahiko Iguchi, Patrick Strefford, and Noah McCormack all teach in the Department of International Relations at Kyoto Sangyo University.

This publication does not differ in content from the book published by BookWay in March 2018.
本書は 2018 年 3 月に BookWay より発行された書籍と内容に相違はありません。

Studying the Human Condition
Science, Human Science, History, Ethics, Arts, Religion

2023年 3 月13日　初版発行

著　者　Russell Garofalo, Masahiko Iguchi,
　　　　Patrick Strefford, Noah McCormack

発行所　学術研究出版（Academic Research Publication）
　　　　〒670-0933　兵庫県姫路市平野町62
　　　　［販売］Tel. 079（280）2727　Fax. 079（244）1482
　　　　［制作］Tel. 079（222）5372
　　　　https://arpub.jp

印刷所　小野高速印刷株式会社
©Noah McCormack 2023, Printed in Japan
ISBN978-4-910733-96-8